Michelle Pfeiffer

By the same author
Burt Lancaster: A Life in Films
Mitchum: The Film Career of Robert Mitchum

Michelle Pfeiffer
A Biography

BRUCE CROWTHER

ROBERT HALE • LONDON

ISBN 0 7090 5226 X

Robert Hale Limited
Clerkenwell House
Clerkenwell Green
London EC1R 0HT

2 4 6 8 10 9 7 5 3 1

Typeset in Palatino by Bookcraft, Stroud, Gloucestershire
Printed in Great Britain by St Edmundsbury Press,
Bury St Edmunds, Suffolk and bound by WBC Bookbinders

Contents

Acknowledgements

As usual I am very grateful, for help in research, to various people, in particular Dave Dalton and Dave Tuck. However, also as usual, all opinions expressed are my own and any errors of fact or judgement which may exist are my responsibility.

BC

Illustrations

Between pages 128 and 129

All illustrations courtesy of Naphine-Walsh Collections

Prologue

From the beginning, Hollywood was a man's town and the motion-picture industry a man's world. No matter that for every leading male actor there was a female counterpart; no matter that women formed a majority of the fast-growing audience for films in those early years. The 'Men Only' signs, unwritten and unspoken though they might be, were imprinted in the minds of everyone who worked in the industry and woe betide anyone who tried to make changes.

But, as in many walks of life, there comes a point beyond which there is no alternative – other than disappearing entirely from the scene – but to fight back.

The female backlash began in the early 1980s and continues into the '90s. It has found at its disposal not only some actresses who had clung on against the odds and advancing years but also a seemingly endless array of highly talented younger women who had been lurking, heaven knows where, until their moment came.

Amongst these actresses were Lauren Bacall, Barbara Hershey, Ann-Margaret, Candice Bergen, Jacqueline Bisset, Diane Keaton, Susan Sarandon, Kathleen Turner, Geena Davis, Theresa Russell, Glenn Close, Debra Winger, Julia Roberts, Holly Hunter, Jessica Lange and Michelle Pfeiffer.

The backlash did not stop with casting; had it done so the movement might have quickly run up against entrenched male concepts and the long-standing domination of Hollywood by sexist ideologues. Fortunately, many of the actresses involved in the new female movement had recognized that part of the problem which beset their counterparts in the past lay in their lack of clout. Now, through careful use of their earnings they built solid financial bases for their own production companies and were prepared to back their own ideas through to realization.

But for a female star like Michelle Pfeiffer to own a production company was one thing, to carry through concepts that were women-orientated needed more than money. It needed perception, collaboration and the support of women in other areas of the film-making process. Apart from female producers, the Hollywood Hills were suddenly alive with the sound of female writers and directors – areas of film-making that had known only a few examples in earlier decades.

For the new wave of screen actresses, and some of their more experienced colleagues who were swept along on the tide of women's films, roles became much more positive. But this was not by any means an all-embracing shift. Men still maintained most of the dominant power bases and continued to call the shots. Consequently, many films still showed women in subordinate roles. This fact prompted Michelle Pfeiffer, in her acceptance speech when receiving the Crystal Award at the 17th Annual Women in Film Luncheon in June 1993, to pointedly address the manner in which women, in films such as *Indecent Proposal*, *Mad Dog and Glory* (both 1993) and *Pretty Woman* (1990), were still being given roles that demeaned womanhood, turning them into chattels, playthings and mindless sex objects.

'So, this is the year of the woman,' Pfeiffer said and then continued ironically, 'Well, yes, it's actually been a good year for women. Demi Moore was sold to Robert Redford for $1 million. Uma Thurman went to Mr De Niro for $40,000 and just three years ago Richard Gere bought Julia Roberts for – what was it? – $3,000? I'd say that was real progress.'

The fact that the Mistress of Ceremonies at the event was Sherry Lansing, producer of *Indecent Proposal*, and Demi Moore was in the audience, shows that Pfeiffer is not prepared to modify her principles to suit her listeners. But then, nothing in her past suggests otherwise.

Entering films as she did in the late 1970s, Michelle Pfeiffer needed only to look around her to know that she was different. In doing so, guided subconsciously by what Hollywood offered as a standard of feminine beauty, she was not impressed with herself. 'I don't know that I've *ever* felt that I was extraordinary looking. In fact, I *know* that I'm not. If anything, I've always felt that I was conventionally pretty, which is an asset in some ways, and in others not. It's a really hard subject to talk about.' Developing this theme on another occasion, she declared, 'I'm not beautiful, Meryl Streep is beautiful. I'm not.' As for sex appeal, she continued, 'I don't have a sex siren's body. I mean, one doesn't say: "Okay, now I'm going to exude sex." One doesn't play sex, just as one doesn't play bored.'

In fact, she was understating her physical attractiveness, which was outstanding long before she entered the motion-picture industry. That attractiveness might have escaped herself but it certainly had not escaped others. The combination of fine yet strong bone structure, porcelain skin and eyes like glistening Wedgwood was something that demanded attention. Undoubtedly, Pfeiffer's appearance opened doors that might well have remained closed had she been merely conventionally pretty. But to enter films riding only on the back of good looks would have spelled disaster.

Speaking of Pfeiffer in this context, director Jonathan Demme remarked that '. . . more than any other beautiful actress, Michelle has been handicapped by her appearance. She has such an overwhelming face that people have cast her because of the way she looks.'

As she subsequently proved in roles like that in *Frankie and Johnny*, Pfeiffer doesn't need the artificial sheen of Hollywood glamour. But it took quite a while for that message to sink in and throughout that time Pfeiffer never lost faith that her abilities would be allowed to surface and that she would ultimately confound those who, consciously or not, downgraded her because of her looks. 'It used to be a handicap. Obviously not an insurmountable one.'

As Demme said: 'I feel . . . that she's been in touch with her gift all along, and that she's exhibited enormous patience with those of us who tend to focus first on how gorgeous she is.'

However, long before *Harper's Bazaar* would name her as one of the ten most beautiful women in America, film-makers had struggled to equate looks with ability.

As for power, that was another field entirely. The meaning of power was something the moguls of early Hollywood understood. They did not understand women. As for the idea that women might be granted power, that was a possibility that seemed never to enter their minds.

Actresses such as Bette Davis, Joan Crawford, Katharine Hepburn and Barbara Stanwyck earned millions of box-office dollars for their employers – and that most certainly earned them respect. But none of these women formed and ran their own production companies. None was allowed to develop and write their own scripts (although Davis reputedly improvised much of her dialogue for *Jezebel* because she was dissatisfied with the script). None ever suggested that they might want to direct their own films; as for directing films with other stars, that was the stuff of dreams.

Yet even the most casual glance at their track records suggests that they all possessed qualities necessary for at least some of these activities. Unfortunately, they lacked the most important quality of all – they were not men.

But the 1980s saw numerous actresses appearing in films in which they had participation over and above that of playing a role on-camera. Although Michelle Pfeiffer had not shown any inclination towards directing a film or bossing a studio, her interest in production was beginning to surface. It would take a little while yet before she came into her own, but the early 1990s would see her become one of Hollywood's most powerful women.

That she should have reached such a high level of achievement and international acceptance and acclaim suggests a very unusual, determined and highly talented young woman.

Michelle Pfeiffer is all of this, and more, and the respect accorded her by her peers is entirely justified. What is remarkable is that she did not decide to attempt a career as an actress until 1978, when she was almost twenty years old.

What happened to this California girl, born on 29 April 1958, is the kind of story Hollywood has been known to invent. In her case, they didn't have to; Michelle Pfeiffer's astonishing success story is true.

1   *The Year of the Woman*

In the wake of countless thousands of Americans, Richard and Donna Pfeiffer, newly married, decided to make the classic move that has entranced their fellow countrymen and women for more than two centuries – they would go west.

So, in the mid-1950s, they left their North Dakota home hoping that they might find a place where they could settle down, find steady work, raise a family, enjoy a little sunshine and, maybe, share in the American Dream. In fact, they went just about as far west as they could go. Midway City, Orange County, California, is just a few miles, along Beach Boulevard, from the Pacific Ocean. Midway City is like many of the other small towns that have been swallowed up to form the immense urban sprawl that has Los Angeles at its centre. Grid-patterned streets, the houses mostly neat little boxes, all perhaps a little drab were it not for the sunshine.

The San Diego Freeway, Interstate 405, bisects Midway City. Travel south along that road, towards San Diego, and in twenty minutes or so the flat urban landscape has given way to the San Joaquin Hills. Travel in the opposite direction and after about forty miles, as the T-Bird flies through the concrete jungle, and that same road swings around to the west of Beverly Hills. And just beyond Beverly Hills lies Hollywood. Literally speaking, that journey isn't difficult – apart from the traffic; take the journey figuratively, from the dull routine of Midway City to the magical world of the movies and it becomes a journey that is the stuff of dreams. Millions have dreamed those dreams, many have attempted to turn dream into reality. Only a few have succeeded.

It wasn't a dream of Dick and Donna Pfeiffer's. He had not

come west to make his name, either in the movies or in any other artistic or show business way; he had come to work and, soon, to raise a family. He started up as a heating and air-conditioning contractor; a job which, in Southern California, is almost as much a sure thing as working in the food chain or the funeral business. As for the family, he and Donna had four children: Richard, Michelle, Lori and DeeDee.

Dick and Donna Pfeiffer had strong ideas about how their children should be raised. They instilled the values of self-sufficiency, of hard work, of honesty and integrity. Michelle Pfeiffer would remember those days with fond affection tinged with an acute awareness that, while they were comfortable, they were not always easy times. She has recalled that her mother encouraged her to be independent, to leave home and stand confidently on her own feet. Donna Pfeiffer never had a career but always wanted her daughter to have one even if it meant postponing marriage. Such lessons, allied to her father's example of hard work – the Protestant work ethic runs deep in the Swiss, Swedish, Dutch and German bloodlines of the Pfeiffer stock – helped develop characteristics that would stand the next Pfeiffer generation in good stead in the world outside Midway City. Amongst other things, Dick Pfeiffer paid his kids fifty cents a time to clean second-hand refrigerators which he planned to recondition and sell.

Not that Michelle had her sights set very high when she was growing up, and certainly they were not set on faraway Hollywood. Indeed, for a while she appeared to have no particular aim in life. She was quite content to drift through school, spending as much time as she could hanging out at Huntington State Beach, the nearest surf-side recreation area which lies just to the south of where Beach Boulevard reaches the ocean.

School was Fountain Valley High School – when she took the trouble to attend classes, that is. After school and at weekends, eager for that self-sufficiency her parents preached, she took part-time jobs. This was from the age of

fourteen onwards – she passed that birthday on 29 April 1972
– but none of these jobs was especially demanding or
gleamed with potential even for the hardest worker. They
were simply a means of providing pocket money and with it
a little of that independence Donna Pfeiffer wanted for her
children.

Michelle's teachers at Fountain Valley High remember her
as being bright enough but an uninterested student, seemingly incapable of the kind of application necessary to advance far academically. Her reading habits in later years
were voracious, leading towards the suspicion that what was
lacking most in her schooldays was intellectual stimulus. If
her teachers could have interested her, she might have been
better at her studies. But she wasn't interested, and she didn't
do better. And who can now say if that was a good or bad
thing – if she had been a better student and had gone on to
higher education might she still have become a film star?

She was thought of at school as a 'wild child'. She remembers herself as being a 'rotten kid. I was always in trouble. I
tried so hard to be good, but I was incapable of it. Just
incapable. With the greatest of effort, I would manage to get
a C in citizenship. I was a bully. I was a tomboy. I used to
beat up all the boys. I was like the mafia don of my school.'
A school report commented that 'I needed to work on my
mouth – I talked too much.'

Most of the time, however, she wasn't at school. She cut
classes and headed for the beach and the surfers where her
teachers' criticism was irrelevant.

For all her waywardness, however, some of the ideas and
ethics her parents had drilled into her had taken root. She
found it impossible to lie to them, even when she had been
up to something she knew would meet with their
disapproval. And she did a lot of things the elder Pfeiffers
had never experienced in their own childhood back in North
Dakota. One time, Michelle stayed away for a few days. 'I
had spent the weekend with all these kids in this un-
chaperoned house – and I knew I was busted. And I came in,

and I forget what kind of lie I told, but I actually burst into tears. I was so shocked at myself!'

Meanwhile, she settled into a string of part-time jobs, including stacking shelves at 4 a.m. in a jeans store at a local shopping mall, working at a small factory where costume jewellery was manufactured, working for an optometrist and being employed at a nursery school. Then came a fairly lengthy spell as an employee of Vons, the huge supermarket chain. There, she would have various duties including working on check-out desks. It was all the same to her, just so long as it filled the time and her bank book. When she had saved enough – with a little help no doubt from her parents – she bought her first car, a cherry-red Mustang, which she promptly wrecked.

She didn't date with the young men employed at Vons. One would recall asking her for a date but 'she said she made it a rule not to go out with anyone from the store'. The boys on the beach, the surfers and sun-worshipping body-builders, were a different proposition although she remained very selective, a little remote, part of but somehow detached from the scene – which at that time included not only surf and sun but also drink and drugs.

When she quit school and began working full-time at Vons, Michelle soon found the undemanding work boring. Remarkably, given the image she offers to the world in the 1990s, she cared little for how she looked. 'I can *see* me standing in the check stand in my little red smock and my black polyester pants and my white nurse shoes. My black pants that had faded to grey, so that my boss was taking up a collection to get me a new pair.'

Deciding on a change, she planned to become a court stenographer and, to this end, took classes at a school in Garden Grove, which lies just to the north of Midway City. That didn't take either and she dropped the idea and the classes and instead tried advancing her education with stints at Golden Valley College but, time after time, she would become bored and drift back to Vons. Life on the check-out might also be boring but it was familiar.

And in between all of this to-ing and fro-ing, she was out at the beach – soaking in the sun, trying out soft drugs, smoking and drinking. And there were the boyfriends; the surfers who viewed their self-centred life through shade-covered eyes eagerly encouraging the attentions of attractive young women which is what Michelle Pfeiffer was fast becoming.

But she was never narcissistic and had no illusions about how she looked. 'I never thought I was attractive to boys . . . I was always beating them up – why should they like me?'

One of her friends, a hairdresser, had different ideas and tried persuading Michelle to take up modelling but she resisted the suggestion because she didn't like the thought of parading herself in front of an audience.

Then one day, at the check-out at Vons, she stood listening to a customer droning on and on about the quality of a cantaloupe. Michelle listened, began a 'what-am-I-doing-here?' chain of thought and ended up asking herself if she could have anything she wanted, what would it be? Later she would regard that moment as a kind of revelation. Suddenly, and with no apparent preamble, she decided that she would try acting. In fact, it wasn't entirely an out-of-nowhere idea. While still at Fountain Valley High she had taken drama classes. Her reason was not that she was interested, but that she had discovered that the system could be manipulated. Drama classes would give her English credits and as the other route involved writing essays on Henry James there was simply no contest. At the moment she made her decision over the alternatives – drama vs deep, complex novels of nineteenth-century manners and mores – she didn't expect to like drama. 'I'd always thought that theatre people were really weird. And I got into this class, and I just fell in love with the people there. They were funny, witty; they were really interesting. It was the only class that I made an effort to go to.'

Even so, the effort she put into drama class was only half-hearted. Her drama teacher at Fountain Valley High, Carole Cooney, remembers that she 'didn't try out for any of the major productions. I saw her as this sunshine surfer beach girl. She was more out of class than in.'

She did make a couple of appearances at the school. One was in a Christmas production, a string of sketches stretched over an entire day. The other was at a history class, run by another teacher, John Bovberg, during which students held a mock trial of former-President Harry S. Truman who was 'charged' with dropping the atomic bomb on Japan. Michelle appeared as a witness for the prosecution, a survivor of the blast, and astonished everyone with her emotional display.

But acting wasn't a career prospect. At least not until the day a large woman in the check-out line at Vons started bitching about a melon.

Suddenly excited and purposeful over her new decision, Michelle did what her hairdresser-friend had been begging her to do; she had photographs taken and promptly entered a beauty contest.

Miss Orange County is a long way from being Miss World but it was a start; and she won. Miss Los Angeles was a much bigger step; but she lost. 'Thank God,' she said later. 'I didn't want to win and be opening drugstores. The reason I went was that I wanted to meet one of the judges, who was a commercial agent.'

For someone who had only just made the decision to attempt a career in show-business, she was already calculatedly setting her sights on the road ahead and developing the kind of tunnel-vision needed for success in certain, perhaps most, enterprises.

But deciding to become an actress and actually making it all the way to Hollywood are two very different matters. For all its high-visibility, Hollywood is a hard place to reach; like a mirage in the desert, it is always there but tantalizingly unreachable. Nevertheless, despite the way in which the image dissolved for so many, just as they thought they had it in their grasp, Hollywood has been a kind of secular Mecca almost since 1913 when the first films were shot there. Good light, needed for the primitive film stock and cameras, and longer days of sunshine which shortened expensive production schedules, made Hollywood an ideal location for the hitherto east-coast-based film industry. It was also a refuge from the Motion Picture Patents Company, the so-called 'Trust', which exercised legally-binding and frequently oppressive watchdog treatment upon film-makers.

Hollywood hung on to its importance for a long time but by the late 1970s, when Michelle Pfeiffer decided it was the place upon which to target her barely nascent career, things had changed. The studios were largely occupied with turning out television programmes. Making films for theatrical release had ceased to be Hollywood's main business. But it was still the place where deals were done, where fortunes might be made or lost, where reputations were created and destroyed. Hollywood was still the place to head, the name to drop, the magic land where dreams might just possibly come true. Even the dreams of a check-out girl at Vons – because Michelle Pfeiffer was being remarkably level-headed despite the heady nature of her plans and ambitions. She decided that she would not quit her job, not just yet. She also knew that deciding to be an actress was one thing, learning the trade was another.

The main thing was, she now had a target in life. Thanks to her parental upbringing, she also had determination and self-assurance. Her education was still lacking, but with remarkable willpower she began to correct that deficiency. Later, she acknowledged 'getting real lost' in the drink and drugs subculture that threatened many young people in Southern California and she would admit how much she had missed by going to the beach and getting stoned. It wasn't that she now wanted simply to catch up with others but that she wanted to do it for herself. She sensed what she had missed and knew that to succeed she had to be much more than just another pretty-faced California girl.

An early reviewer hinted that she might be another candidate for 'bimbo limbo' and that must certainly have been a danger. Had she lacked the determination to succeed she might well have settled for what others thought she was capable of; which, by and large, wasn't very much. Many people in Hollywood lacked the perception to see past the blue-eyed, blonde good looks, the slender and shapely body. Conditioned by heaven knows how many thousands of would-be female movie stars who had come to Hollywood with pretty faces, good bodies and no talent, they saw nothing special in Michelle Pfeiffer.

In fact, her distinctive features, which echo the Pfeiffer northern-European stock, are very different from those of the surf-bunnies of Southern California. She has an enviable bone structure even if she is dismissive of herself. 'I look like a duck,' she frequently says, perhaps out of embarrassment at being complimented on her appearance. Other times, as a variation on the theme, she says she walks like a duck and worries about her hands ('they're too long') or some other real or imagined feature that doesn't fit the stereotype. But a stereotype was the last thing she wanted to be.

Talking to Leslie Bennetts of *Vanity Fair* some years later she commented upon the combination of parental upbringing and goofing-off from school which had created her character at the time she moved out of Midway City and attempted to break into films. 'I'm really glad now that I had that rebellious spirit. I think it's one of the biggest influences on my success. It's why I moved away from home. It's the thing that gave me the courage to move to Los Angeles and enter such a foreign world that I was completely unprepared for.'

Maybe she wasn't prepared for the foreign world of Hollywood, certainly Hollywood wasn't prepared for her and, as has happened so often to hopeful actresses in the past, for the first couple of years there was always the danger that the blindness of others would prove an insurmountable obstacle. Fortunately, she was tough enough to make them change their minds.

2 *From Hot Pants to Hot Property*

Some measure of the determination with which Michelle Pfeiffer began her acting career can be gained from the fact that she had to overcome the negative responses of many of those around her.

Her father discouraged her, believing that the notion was merely juvenile fantasy. A former teacher, John Bovberg, saw her a couple of years after she left school and was still working in the local supermarket. When she eagerly told him of her plans to become an actress he recommended that she should go back to school to attain further qualifications. Even so, he remembers that 'she seemed driven; she seemed to have a lot of confidence'. Her high-school drama teacher, although closer to the potential, would later admit that she had dismissed Pfeiffer as just another 'surfer chick'. If Pfeiffer truly had been just another air-headed beach blonde she might well have been discouraged by such attitudes but she was made of much sterner stuff. She acquired an agent, John LaRocca, and began taking acting lessons but wisely stayed with Vons, working at a branch closer to Hollywood.

LaRocca helped her obtain her Screen Actors' Guild card and she began auditioning for television commercials. In order to be a good commercial actor, she observes, 'you have to learn how to do a specific kind of bad acting well. If you walk out of an audition feeling like you made an asshole of yourself, chances are you got the job.'

LaRocca also landed her her first tiny one-line part in a television series, *Fantasy Island*. The series, which ran for approximately 120 episodes from 1977 until 1982, starred

Ricardo Montalban, the Mexican-born actor whose best work was on Broadway and television – Hollywood inevitably typecast him as a 'Latin lover'. In *Fantasy Island*, Montalban played the owner of an island where visitors could live out their fantasies at $10,000 a time.

Pfeiffer's episode was made and first-screened as long ago as 1979, but she can still remember the occasion and the line with complete clarity. 'I'll never forget it, "Who is he, Naomi?" I practised and practised that line. I remember being so discombobulated, because I had to find my mark – you know, you don't learn that in acting class. And the lights were so bright I couldn't keep my eyes open. I remember showing up for work and my name was on the dressing room door.'

Although *Fantasy Island* might appear to be a tiny beginning when viewed from the vantage point of her acceptance as an international superstar, it was a precarious toe-hold on the ladder. There was still a long way to go and her next role might well have killed off her career almost before she had time to make an impact.

Typically casting her for her looks alone, she was given an unnamed role, known only as 'The Bombshell', in a television series, *Delta House*, a spin-off from John Landis's 1978 film, *National Lampoon's Animal House*. The film, which starred John Belushi, Canadian-born actors John Vernon and Donald Sutherland, and Bruce McGill, had been successful with its simplistic premise, a string of anecdotal comedy sketches hung loosely around the antics of a college fraternity, the Delta House. The film's humour was both predictable and unimaginatively vulgar, yet managed at times to be very funny. Nevertheless, the film had pretty much used up the potential and the television series was left to wearily recycle well-worn situations and gags. The series starred Peter Fox and Stephen Furst with Bruce McGill reprising his role from the original film. Years later, McGill was asked about Pfeiffer's appearances in *Delta House*. He remembers that she 'was absolutely unschooled as an actress, but she was always asking the right questions.' McGill then went on to use a phrase which went into just about every subsequent newspaper and magazine piece about her. 'She was drop-dead gorgeous, of course.'

Wearing tight clothes with a padded bra, Pfeiffer had little to do but look 'drop-dead gorgeous' only rarely being granted a few lines. She knew that this was not what she wanted. 'I used to call up my agent, crying on the phone: "They're putting me in hot pants again."' She worried over what impression she might be making. 'Here we were, pre-senting me like I was this sexy thing and I was thinking, "What if people don't think I'm sexy? I'm going to look stupid."'

But her agent was trying hard to improve the quality of the roles that might be offered to his new and inexperienced client. While she was working on *Delta House*, LaRocca se-cured roles for her in two films. The first was the small role of Tricia in a made-for-television drama entitled *The Solitary Man* (1979), starring Earl Holliman and Carrie Snodgrass. Holliman was now fifty and had previously played support-ing roles, often in westerns, and was currently appearing in the popular television series *Police Woman*. Snodgrass, who was Oscar-nominated for her first film, *Diary of a Mad House-wife* (1970), had only recently returned to work after several years outside show business. The story of *The Solitary Man* follows the break-up of a family and the psychological dis-integration of the husband when his wife announces that she wants a divorce after eighteen years of marriage. Sombre, but honest, the storyline, which is traced from the husband's point-of-view, bears some similarities to that of the same year's (but later) *Kramer vs Kramer*.

The second of the two films made while Pfeiffer was in a *Delta House* was *Falling in Love Again* (1980) which received some good notices. Importantly for Pfeiffer, so did she.

The film tells the story of Harry Lewis (Elliott Gould), owner of a Los Angeles fashion store run by his wife, Sue (Susannah York). Harry greets the onset of middle age by fondly reminiscing about his youth and his almost-forgotten dreams. With his marriage at a low ebb, Harry takes his wife and two teenaged children across country to New York where he plans to attend a high-school-class reunion.

In flashback, young Harry (Stuart Paul), is a poor Jew living in the Bronx with his parents (Robert Hackman and Kay Ballard). Harry sets his career sights on becoming an architect but also has his eyes on Sue Wellington (Pfeiffer), the daughter of a rich WASP (White Anglo-Saxon Protestant) family. Despite the fact that Sue's father (Herbert Rudley) is his father's employer, Harry is determined to win her. He is helped in his endeavours by a match-making friend, Stan the Con (Steven Paul), and the willing co-operation of a bored housewife, Cheryl Herman (Cathy Tolbert), who initiates him into sex.

Gradually, Sue is won over. For one thing, Harry makes her laugh and he is given to romantic gestures such as climbing a tree to reach her window and deliver her favourite cookies. But marriage to Sue does more than achieve a goal for Harry; it also ends his career ambitions.

Back in the present, the class reunion goes well and helps Harry rethink his life, but it also causes him embarrassment. At one point, he tells some of his former classmates what he really wanted to do with his life and how everything has gone wrong. So intent is he on recounting his disappointments that he fails to notice that his wife is standing near and hears everything.

The story ends happily, it's that kind of film, with Harry and Sue once again seeing one another as they were and not as the strangers they have become.

Performances are generally strong, with Gould accurately capturing the attitude of a man whose life is filled with uncertainties and the vague unease that he has left it too late to achieve anything. British actress Susannah York is also very good in her role as the wife who has watched her husband decline but who at first cannot find the way to handle the problem.

Although predictable and awash with clichés, *Falling In Love Again* is done well and for this much credit must go to director Steven Paul, then aged only twenty, who made a notable debut. Indeed, the film might be described as a labour of love by the Paul family. Steven not only directed the film but also played the role of the matchmaker. The story was by Steven and his father, Hank. Steven's brother, Stuart, plays Harry as a young man; his father was executive producer and helped raise the $3 million budget; his mother, Dorothy Koster Paul, was associate producer and casting director, his sister, Bonnie, plays one of grown-up Harry's children; and there is also a Cheri Paul credited as props mistress.

All this enterprise, and the fact that the result is enjoyable, if lightweight, entertainment, deserved a better fate than the film received. Pfeiffer attracted critical attention, with *Variety* declaring that she 'makes a strong impression . . . with a dreamy look in her eyes which is quite distinctive'. Joe Bradley, in *Films and Filming*, thought her 'very promising' and speculated (this was a year or so after the film's release) that her presence might help the film if her career took off. But her career didn't take off, at least not in time to help *Falling in Love Again*. The film failed to secure a theatrical release and, instead, was launched with scant ceremony on to the video circuit with its title shortened to *In Love*.

Pfeiffer's next role, in *The Hollywood Knights* (1980), was scarcely a step upwards. Set in California in 1965, the story follows the supposedly comical activities of a group of moronic teenagers when, on Halloween, they take revenge on some Beverly Hills residents who have had a local diner closed down over the protests of the young people who hang out there.

Aimed at the juvenile audience, the film catalogues activities which seldom rise above the puerile. Scrawling obscenities on walls and urinating into a punch-bowl doesn't even sound like fun. And it isn't. Pfeiffer, who plays the role of Suzie-Q, a car-hop, gets to wear hot pants again, and rates only ninth billing. Even further down the cast list is Tony Danza, who would make his name in television sit-coms such as *Taxi* and *Who's the Boss?*

Variety was scathing (but fortunately didn't mention Pfeiffer), categorizing the film as a 'compendium of gross-outs as avoidable as drive-in food'. As for the film's structure, or lack of it, this critic went on to state that 'experiencing this 90-minute paean to jerkdom is akin to sitting in a car while someone else is punching up different stations on the AM band.'

About this and her next film, Pfeiffer commented that even if they 'weren't exactly what I ideally wanted, each time I made a choice, I made sure it was something a little better than the last one'.

Well, not quite. The other film also foundered very badly on the rocks of critical disdain and public apathy. This time, however, she was in a big-budget, multi-starring vehicle, a fact which made its failure even more disappointing for all concerned.

Charlie Chan and the Curse of the Dragon Queen (1980) got off to an unpromising start when a large section of the population of San Francisco took exception to it before a single frame was exposed. Set and shot in San Francisco, the film revived the famous Chinese detective of long-ago Hollywood, casting Peter Ustinov in the leading role. Despite the multi-lingual actor's multi-ethnic background, he is no Chinaman. Even the fact that the villainous Dragon Queen is an Occidental (she is played by Angie Dickinson) didn't do much to placate the city's irate Orientals. They picketed the locations and boycotted the finished film. In the event, the film's makers might well have wished they'd taken the hint and dropped the production.

The earnest simplicity of the 1930s and '40s Chan films was rather endearing in a low-key manner. They didn't have Chinese actors in the leading role either but offered solid B-picture entertainment. In the expensive star-studded revival, director Clive Donner and screenwriters Stan Burns

and David Axelrod went for high camp and juvenile slap-
stick.

The story aimlessly follows Chan's grandson, Lee (Richard Hatch), who takes centre stage in his attempts to outdo
his famous grandfather. Lee's fiancée is WASP princess Cor-
delia Farington III (Pfeiffer) who is one of many lightweight
background figures to an overly complicated and very
creaky plot. Lee is attempting to solve a series of bizarre
murders in San Francisco's Chinatown. Alongside all this,
Lee and Charlie attempt to lift a curse placed on their family
many years ago by the Dragon Queen when Charlie unmasked her as the killer of her lover, Bernie Lupowitz.

Eventually, after many pseudo-comic chases, the Dragon
Queen is again sent off to prison but Charlie has now discovered that the new series of murders were carried out by Mrs
Lupowitz (Lee Grant). She hates Charlie for forcing a public
scandal at the time of her husband's death, and has staged
the murders to make him look foolishly inept as he struggles
to solve them.

A sequence in a film theatre where an 'old' Charlie Chan
movie is being screened, which confuses the killer, doesn't
work even half as well as the similar, but excellently-realized,
sequence in *Targets*, Peter Bogdanovich's 1968 film, starring
Boris Karloff as a retired horror-film actor who pursues a
real-life killer through a drive-in movie theatre. Donner's
re-working of the idea might be homage; or it might just be
lack of imagination.

Other blurred reflections of old Hollywood come in the
shape of Mrs Dangers (Rachel Roberts), doing a turn as
Rebecca's Mrs Danvers, and Roddy McDowall, as Gillespie
the butler, sending up wheelchair-bound Lionel Barrymore
in the old Dr Kildare films.

The talents of Ustinov, Dickinson, McDowall, Grant and
Roberts (in her last film role) are wasted as are those of Brian
Keith and Johnny Sekka. Grant's career was especially un-
fortunate, beginning spectacularly in 1951 with the Best Actress Award at the Cannes Film Festival and an unsuccessful

Oscar nomination for *Detective Story*. She then promptly fell foul of the McCarthy witchhunt and hardly worked at all in films or television until the early 1960s. She won the 1975 Best Supporting Actress Oscar for *Shampoo*. Roberts' best work was on the stage but she had some good film roles, being nominated for a Best Actress Oscar for *This Sporting Life* (1963).

London-born McDowall was a child star of the late 1930s and early '40s. As an adult he kept his career alive in films and, increasingly, in television but often had to make do with shallow roles which he either built up or, as here, sent up wildly. Dickinson's career also had its ups and downs, at the time she was playing the lead in the very popular television series, *Police Woman*.

Despite all the film's many flaws and unhappy reviews, Pfeiffer didn't do too badly with *Variety* singling her out for perceptive praise: 'Given the lack of competition, it is no wonder that newcomer Michelle Pfeiffer steals what little is up for grabs in the film. Much like Goldie Hawn, Pfeiffer has a wacky, fey way about her that's bound to be put to better use in the future.'

Variety's comment was prescient but there were hurdles to overcome, not least in the likening to Hawn. Comparisons like this rarely help an actress or actor striving for recognition. In this case, the comparison was also off-the-mark. Even in the early stages of her career, Pfeiffer never resorted to the wide-eyed helplessness that was Hawn's trademark.

For all the slow but steady progress of her career, Pfeiffer's private life had begun to drift. She still drank and smoked and occasionally did soft drugs. None of them to excess, except perhaps the smoking, but neither was any of this helping her. Realizing the dangers, she quit everything and in seeking a straight path became involved with what she would later describe vaguely as a vegetarian-metaphysical cult. California is awash with quasi-religious, quasi-philo-sophical, quasi-you-name-it-they've-got-it groups which exercise various forms of control. Control over mind, body, psyche and, usually, money.

On the rare occasions when she has discussed this period, Pfeiffer admitted to feeling a need to have someone in control of her life but that this particular venture was a bad and expensive mistake. In the long run she would still need control over her life and career but eventually discovered that she had the strength of mind to do this herself.

She was involved with the cult for almost two years but spent the last months of the association trying unsuccessfully to break away. Fortunately, she had met a young man at her acting classes, Peter Horton, and he helped her. Horton had a role in a film about a cult and the manner in which mind-control was exercised; conversations with Horton led to Pfeiffer making the break she knew was necessary. With his help, she left the cult and she and Horton became firm friends, then lovers. Although she was unsure about marriage to anyone, least of all an actor, this was the direction in which their relationship began to move.

This time also saw Pfeiffer making a reassessment of her career which led to another break, this time with her agent.

John LaRocca had worked hard for her and she was grateful but believed she could do better if she signed with a bigger agency. LaRocca clearly didn't agree, finding it difficult to talk about the break even years later. But Pfeiffer knew what she wanted which was to be a client of the giant William Morris Agency. She signed with them where she was handled by Gary Lucchesi and Alan Iezman.

Nevertheless, work had been steady with LaRocca and throughout 1981 she was still involved in television projects he had secured for her.

She went into a series produced by Aaron Spelling and Douglas S. Cramer for ABC. The series was about a unit of the Los Angeles Police Department with the somewhat laboured label, the Burglary Auto Detail, Commercial Auto Thefts, the initials of which went to form the series title, *B.A.D. Cats*. The series starred Steven Hanks and Asher

Brauner as Ocee James and Nick Donovan, two ex-stock car racing drivers who are now cops. Most of the screentime followed this pair through innumerable highly improbable car chases. Pfeiffer was back-up cop, 'Sunshine' Samantha Jensen, and other regulars were Vic Morrow, as Captain Skip, and Jimmie Walker as Rodney Washington, a repo man who is also a police informer. The series debuted on 4 January 1980 but closed after only six 60-minute episodes.

Other television work included an appearance in *Splendor in the Grass*. This is the story of two young people, Bud Stampler and Deanie Loomis, growing up and discovering love in a small mid-Western town in the 1920s. William Inge's stage play was first filmed in 1961 with Warren Beatty and Natalie Wood in the leading roles, Inge writing the screenplay for which he won an Oscar. The NBC television version, which is a scene-by-scene remake of the theatrical version of the play, stars Cyril O'Reilly and Melissa Gilbert as the young lovers. Pfeiffer plays Ginny, Bud's wild young sister.

Next came *Callie and Son* in which Pfeiffer was fifth-billed in the small role of Sue Lynn. This television film, a starring vehicle for television's 'Bionic Woman', Lindsay Wagner, is the story of a dirt-poor young waitress who marries a millionaire newspaper tycoon and then uses her new-found riches to find and reclaim her illegitimate son. Well made, and with strong support from Dabney Coleman, the film was well received and Pfeiffer's contribution, although small, was noticed.

In *The Children Nobody Wanted* Pfeiffer moved up to co-star billing with Frederic Lehne. She plays Jennifer Williams, a nurse who is the girlfriend of Tom Butterfield. The story was based upon the real-life Butterfield's efforts to provide care for mentally-handicapped children. Butterfield, a teenager at the time, met a young boy, Joey, played in the film by Joe Turly, who was held in a mental institution although, in fact, normal. Butterfield promptly began a determined fight against authority and eventually became, at nineteen, the youngest foster-parent in American history. With at first nine boys in his care, he went on to found the Butterfield Youth Ranches of Missouri. Butterfield, who was associate producer of the film, died shortly after the film was transmitted.

Pfeiffer also tested herself on the stage, appearing in *Playground in the Fall*, a small-scale production staged in Los Angeles. This led to nothing else of a similar nature but it was all good training. She was also eagerly learning all that she could about her craft and studied everything that happened in the television studios where she worked. The more she knew, she reasoned, the better she would become and, even more important, the more she could control her career.

Her relationship with Horton was also developing and they were married without fuss in Santa Monica.

Meanwhile, Pfeiffer's new agents had been attempting to land her a big role in a big film. The film on which they had set their sights was a planned sequel to the 1978 musical *Grease*.

On 14 February 1972, *Grease* began life as an off-Broadway show. Written by Jim Jacobs and Warren Casey and starring Barry Bostwick, Adrienne Barbeau, Timothy Meyers and Carole Demas, the show was set in the world of high-school students in the 1950s. Although New York's theatre critics were a little sniffy (they were, after all, the wrong generation to feel nostalgic about early rock 'n' roll), the show developed a following. Before the year was out it had moved on to Broadway where it ran and ran, eventually clocking up 3,388 performances. 1n 1994, a revival of *Grease* was back on Broadway.

Ignoring the advice of just about everyone, film producer Allan Carr bought the screen rights and saw his judgement vindicated. Starring John Travolta and Olivia Newton-John, the film earned Carr a fortune. Now, Carr planned to do it all again and, following the 1970s penchant for making sequels to just about anything that more than broke even at the box-office, he called his new venture *Grease 2*.

Slated to direct the film was Patricia Birch and she later

recalled Pfeiffer's audition. 'She sort of wandered in very late in the day and she was just kind of delectable. I liked her right away . . . she didn't think she could dance, but she moved beautifully. And she could *act*.'

Pfeiffer remembers the audition a little differently, stating that going to it was a fluke but that, 'somehow, through the process of going back and dancing, and then going back and singing, I ended up getting the part.' She was up for the female lead and her test was with one of the actors who failed to land the male lead. She had strong competition, including Lisa Hartman and rock star Pat Benatar, but she made a big impression and her honeymoon with her new husband was interrupted by a call from her agents. She had got the part.

Set in 1961, *Grease 2* (1982) centres on a group of students at Rydell High. Recently arrived from England is Michael Carrington (Maxwell Caulfield) and although warned off by his cousin, Frenchy (Didi Conn), he is greatly attracted to Stephanie Zinone (Pfeiffer) although she barely notices him. Stephanie is the leader of a sorority, the Pink Ladies, who include Frenchy, Paulette Rebchuck (Lorna Luft, the daughter of Sid Luft and Judy Garland), Sharon Cooper (Maureen Teefy) and Rhonda Ritter (Alison Price). The Pink Ladies customarily hang out with a motor-cycle fraternity, the T-Birds, who are led by Johnny Nogarelli (Adrian Zmed). Traditionally, the Pink Ladies' leader and the T-Birds' leader date but Stephanie is weary of Johnny who is, anyway, being pursued by Paulette. Michael helps pay his school fees by writing essays for the T-Birds for whom biking is much more important than studying. With his surplus earnings, Michael buys motor-cycle parts and eventually builds his own machine.

A rival motor-cycle gang, the Cycle Lords, cause problems but Michael, masked and mysterious, outrides them and attracts Stephanie's attention. She climbs on to the pillion of his machine, thus breaking a T-Bird/Pink Lady rule. Michael is then chased away and driven off the road, presumably to his death. Stephanie's true feelings for the mystery man surface but somehow she sings her way through the end-of-term show. She and Johnny jointly win the talent contest but then the Cycle Lords reappear and break up the celebrations. Suddenly, the mysterious masked rider reappears, driving off the interlopers before revealing his real identity to Stephanie. The pair are united in their love and Michael is admitted to the T-Bird fraternity.

Despite the rather lame premise and the wearily predictable storyline, there was no reason why *Grease 2* should not have been a success. There were, however, numerous problems lying in wait for the unwary and inexperienced. The film was Birch's debut as a director although she had worked on *Grease* (stage and film) as choreographer and also choreographed the sequel. Perhaps as a result of this background, the non-musical scenes are stodgily presented. Unfortunately, the film's pacing is also off and too many of the musical numbers come in clumps. The music, too, was generally forgettable and did not have any hit songs, unlike the original which had 'Hopelessly Devoted to You' and 'You're the One That I Want'. Adding to the film's structural burdens, a dream sequence, in which Stephanie imagines a bikers' heaven piled high with neatly stacked riderless motor-cycles, is tackily sentimental.

Tossed into the film, more as token adults than with real parts to play, are veteran comedian Sid Caesar, as Coach Calhoun (a role he played in *Grease*), and the wonderfully acerbic screen comedienne Eve Arden. As schoolteacher Miss McGee, Arden does her best but even she has a hard time with moments like the one where a girl student embarrassedly whispers, 'I missed my last two periods' and Arden gaily replies, 'That's all right, dear, you can make them up after school.'

Also involved, but only briefly (as teachers Mr Stuart and Miss Mason), are a couple of minor idols of the decade in which the film is set: Tab Hunter and Connie Stevens.

As the film's leads, Pfeiffer and Caulfield are a decidedly mixed pair. She is outgoing and filled with vibrant sexuality, which is in marked contrast to the fragile charm of Newton-John in the first film; he displays very little charisma, although having to play his character's most dynamic moments masked by crash helmet and goggles can't have been easy. Reputedly, Pfeiffer and Caulfield did not hit it off despite the film's publicity which offered them as a joint hot property, and the director's claim that she 'knew the chemistry would be good between [them]'.

Reviews of the film were almost unanimous in their condemnation of its flaws and hardly anyone escaped unscathed. Richard Schickel, in *Time*, referring in passing to the first film, wrote, 'Once again, the cheeky, satirical spirit that animated the big Broadway show has been dispensed with ... *Grease 2* has assembled bloodless pastiches of 20-year-old pop music, reduced antique dance styles to their simplest components, ignored the authentic texture of language, manners and style except for the most obvious elements. The story is of the same calibre ... Pfeiffer is pretty and has a certain spirit about her, but the vacant Caulfield is surely the least promising newcomer since Pia Zadora.'

Geoff Brown, in *Monthly Film Bulletin*, thought that 'the two lifeless leads hog the close-ups to little effect; spirited supporting players like Maureen Teefy and Lorna Luft meanwhile have to struggle for breathing space.' Simon Button, in *Films*, was somewhat happier with the leads, declaring that their acting 'is well up to the mark. But what we don't get is star quality. They may have it, and a couple of scenes they share hint at it, but it would take a director of more experience than neophyte Patricia Birch to bring it out.'

Variety singled out Pfeiffer for some near-praise: 'Gorgeous Michelle Pfeiffer plays the leader of the foxy Pink Ladies ... [and] is all anyone could ask for in the looks department, and ... she fills Newton-John's shoes and tight pants very well, thank you.' Sally Hibbin, in *Films and Filming*, thought that Pfeiffer played her role 'with attractive guilelessness' but John Marriott, in *Films (on Screen and Video)*, called hers 'a walk-through performance'. Barry Wigmore, in London's *Daily Mirror*, commented that the backers of the film were pinning their hopes of returns like those of *Grease* on a 'slender Californian girl with long blonde hair and wide blue eyes'.

Such financial aspirations were not entirely fruitless. For all the critical disdain, the film did make money although most of the returns came from worldwide distribution rather than within the borders of the USA. Unfortunately, the parochialism of Hollywood is such that *Grease 2* was therefore regarded as a financial failure and most of those associated with it were shunned, at least for a time.

For Pfeiffer, it proved to be a very bad hiccup in the progress of her career. Conflicting claims about the next year have been made. Her former agent, John LaRocca, stated baldly: 'She couldn't get any jobs. Nobody wanted to hire her.' Pfeiffer maintained that roles were offered but were more of the same, hot-panted sexy young women, and she wanted better than that.

In this she was supported by her acting teacher, Peggy Feury, who recommended that she should raise her sights. But this was something easier said than done.

Throughout its history, Hollywood has been a hard place for women to succeed. Customarily, they have been outweighed by men in most areas of film-making, except on the screen. Even there, women usually had to take second billing and were, anyway, directed by men.

Patricia Birch, Pfeiffer's director on *Grease 2*, was in a position to know the obstacles. As a woman in what was, even in the early 1980s, still regarded as a man's job, she had to fight just to be recognized. She spotted some important qualities in the young actress which she knew were invaluable. 'She's like a little racehorse. She has both a delicacy and a strong will.'

Pfeiffer would have to discover within herself that strong will. Many before her had tried to buck the Hollywood system, not many had succeeded.

3   Firepower, Fantasy and Fun

Hollywood's part-time preoccupation with churning out sequels to money-spinning films (*Jaws*, *Rambo*, *Rocky*, *Alien*, etcetera) has a close cousin in its habit of remaking distinguished predecessors.

The reasons why Brian De Palma chose to remake Scarface in 1983 appear to be rather more complex than most. The original *Scarface* (1932) became an overnight sensation and an enduring classic even if latter-day viewings raise rather a lot of questions about its true merits.

Based very loosely upon the real-life gang lord, 'Scarface' Al Capone, the 1932 version was directed by Howard Hawks from a multi-authored screenplay by, amongst others, Ben Hecht and W. R. Burnett. What helped give this *Scarface* its enormous initial impact was that Capone was still a force to be reckoned with; gangsters like him (in the film he becomes 'Tony Camonte' in a manic portrayal by Paul Muni) were everywhere, especially in the streets of Chicago and New York City.

An important factor in the film's success was its urgent, topical, look and sound. As the programme notes commented when the film was revived at London's National Film Theatre in 1961, 'Because it was so close to the actual events, it possesses a kind of newsreel quality which cannot be recaptured or imitated. It vibrates with the impact of things that were real and deeply felt.'

These remarks carry a warning but Brian De Palma, confident in his ability to recapture real moments of action deeply felt by the contemporary audience, chose to ignore it.

In interviews, De Palma has insisted that violence is an

important and frequently integral part of film-making and holds the view that public fears of violence in the streets being prompted by violent films are unsupported by reality. In his approach to *Scarface*, however, De Palma seems to have opposing views on different aspects of the film's message. On the one hand, the almost non-stop violence, with fists, knives, chainsaws and an astonishing array of firepower from handguns to grenade launchers, he regards as non-influential. On the other hand, he has expressed the hope that the film might be a means of deflecting young people from becoming addicted to drugs.

What comes through the tumultuous violence of the film is a barely veiled suggestion that however bloody and squalid the life of the drug dealer might be, it's better than being dirt-poor and starving painfully on the streets of conspicuously affluent cities.

Perhaps the greatest weakness lies in public perceptions of criminals. In the 1930s the urban gangsters were guardedly, if mistakenly, admired. Their close cousins, rural bandits like John Dillinger, were, in contrast, championed by the public whatever the FBI might have thought to the contrary in their labelling of 'Public Enemies'. Today's drug barons, dealers and pushers do not hold the same place in public esteem.

For all its faults, *Scarface* (1983) attracted a great deal of attention and it was an excellent showcase for Michelle Pfeiffer to present a different image to the film world. She had to work very hard to land the role, auditioning twice before overcoming De Palma's apparent indifference. Perhaps, even at that stage, the director was aware that this was to be a film in which women had only peripheral roles to play.

In *Scarface*, one of the criminals bundled out of Cuba when Fidel Castro, the island's president, agreed to allow some 125,000 'refugees' to sail to Florida where they had been granted conditional asylum by the US government, is Tony 'Scarface' Montana. Immoral, ill-educated, cold, calculating and irredeemably violent, Tony (Al Pacino) and his friend,

Manny Ray (Steven Bauer), are housed in a Florida intern-
ment camp where their backgrounds are checked by dis-
mayed government officials to whom Tony happily explains
how he comes to speak such 'good' English. 'My father ta'
me to the movies. I watch the guys li' Humphrey Bogar',
James Cagney, I learn to spe' from those guys. I li' those
guys.'

Word comes to Tony and Manny that their release can be
engineered in return for a favour; they must kill another
internee, a genuine political exile, Rebenga (Roberto Con-
treras). The task, no problem for Tony, is quickly carried out
under cover of an artificially staged riot, and soon the two
petty and vicious criminals are on their way to what they
confidently expect will be freedom and better things.

In fact, the first things are not much better and only
marginally freer; Tony and Manny are obliged to take menial
jobs at a taco stand. The unlovely pair quickly tire of their
legitimate work and eagerly take on a contract offered them
by Omar (F. Murray Abraham) to deliver money to a group
of Colombian drug-runners in return for a shipment of cocaine. Recruiting a handful of friends, including Angel (Pepe
Serna), they meet with the Colombians but are double-
crossed in a bloody encounter in which Angel is hideously
murdered. Tony and Manny shoot their way out of the trap
(in the process Tony's life is saved by Manny), taking with
them both the money and the cocaine.

Inspired by a sky-writing airplane which extols the promise that 'The world is yours', Tony believes that nothing can
stop him and for a while it appears as though he is right.

Omar is lieutenant to the local crime lord, Frank Lopez
(Robert Loggia), and Tony and Manny become a part of the
organization. Sent to Bolivia with Omar to conclude a deal
with drug baron Alejandro Sosa (Paul Shenar), Tony takes
control of the negotiations and sits quietly by as Sosa arranges for Omar's execution; he is dropped from a helicopter.

Now allied with Sosa, Tony returns to Florida and begins
his inexorable climb to take over Lopez's empire. His next

actions follow the credo announced by Tony Camonte in the original *Scarface*: 'I'm going to run the whole works. There's only one law: Do it first, do it yourself, and keep on doing it.' Setting his sights not only on Lopez but also on his mistress, Elvira (Pfeiffer), Tony's behaviour angers his boss who tries to assert his crumbling authority through his own people and through the actions of a crooked cop, Bernstein (Harris Yulin). Tony refuses to be intimidated and Lopez sends two hitmen to assassinate him. Wounded, Tony survives and retaliates violently, killing both Lopez and Bernstein. Now in complete control of the organization, he marries Elvira, whose drug habit has already turned her into a barren, coldly aloof, zombie.

Now that he has achieved his ambition ('I want what's comin' to me – the world an' everythin' in it'), Tony decides to visit his mother and sister Gina (Miriam Colon and Mary Elizabeth Mastrantonio), who are already poor but legitimate residents in the city. His mother is openly antagonistic to her son but Tony's sister, grown into a voluptuous young woman since he last saw her, clearly idolizes him.

As Tony's power and wealth increase, he retreats into closely guarded isolation; Elvira drifts silently from his life and Tony is entrapped by agents of the Drugs Enforcement Agency. Only the intervention of Sosa saves him from prison, but at a price. Tony must help set up the assassination of a delegate to the United Nations whose drugs-busting activities are increasingly threatening Sosa and his fellow drug barons. Tony travels to New York but aborts the plan to blow up the delegate's limousine when he discovers that the bombing will also kill the man's family. When the assassin, sent along by Sosa to plant the remote-controlled bomb, objects and verbally abuses Tony, he is shot.

Back in Miami, Tony decides to visit his sister for whom he has developed a deep, incestuous passion. Although he had previously warned Manny against becoming familiar with Gina, Tony discovers that the two are living together. Enraged, he kills Manny only to hear his sister screaming that she and Manny were not only in love but were married that day and had happily planned to surprise him.

Tony locks himself away in his mansion to await the arrival of an army of gunmen sent by Sosa with orders to kill him. One by one, Tony's bodyguards are killed and so, too, are dozens of Sosa's men. Tony sits waiting in his study, watching events on closed-circuit television while snorting up colossal amounts of cocaine.

As the invaders enter the house and make their way towards the study, Gina, who now understands her brother's illicit passion for her, enters the room and flaunts herself at Tony, screaming, 'Fuck me! Fuck me! Fuck me!'

Distracted, Tony fails to see one of the invaders clamber over the balcony and enter the room behind him but the man's shots hit Gina before Tony kills him. Taking a grenade launcher from the gun cabinet, Tony leaves the study and from the upper hallway kills one after another of the surviving assassins but, finally, the leader of the group, who has also entered the study by way of the balcony, walks up behind him and empties both barrels of a shotgun into his back.

Tony crashes through the balustrade and into the ornamental pool which occupies the lower hallway and which contains a garish statuette of a globe bearing the words Tony adopted as his motto: 'The world is yours'.

Given the storyline, which concentrates upon the character of Tony Montana, it was important that a strong actor should be cast in the role. The choice of Al Pacino was not only satisfactory because the actor had the strength to sustain the role and looked the part, but also because he brought with him inevitable echoes of his performance as Michael Corleone in *The Godfather* (1972) and *The Godfather, Part Two* (1974) – the latter an example of a sequel which was largely justified by its developing concept (and which, incidentally, worked beautifully when, some years later, it was recut with the first film to form a sequential storyline for transmission on television).

Pacino makes Tony Montana a thoroughly detestable individual which contrasts vividly with Paul Muni's Tony Camonte in the 1932 version whose characterization was almost endearing through the actor's wild mugging.

Pacino's presence necessarily evokes memories of the two *Godfather* films but, despite the fact that they deal with organized crime, there are no real similarities. Most important of the differences is the fact that in the hands of writer-director Francis Ford Coppola, the activities of the Corleone family become a somewhat unsettling hymn of praise for the American Way of Life (and Death). Pacino's character, in *Scarface*, and De Palma's approach to Oliver Stone's screenplay, which is credited as being 'suggested by' the earlier version, are both much less assured than Coppola's. More realistically or at least with greater moral justification – they give Scarface no redeeming features whatsoever (until, that is, his somewhat out-of-character refusal to kill the UN delegate's family).

One hinted similarity between the two characters comes in the manner in which Pacino's playing of Tony Montana begins with an arrogant vitality which descends into insane homicidal depths as the film develops. As Michael Corleone, Pacino begins as a happy non-criminal member of the family only to sink into the depths of implacable evil as the films progress, a process which continues its descent through the final episode of Coppola's trilogy.

The concentration upon Tony, allied to Pacino's powerful performance, meant that every other character became a minor role and every other actor and actress was faced with the need to produce something special. Fortunately, several of them did and thus helped prevent the film from toppling over and becoming merely a one-man show.

Among the male actors worth noting are F. Murray Abraham, Harris Yulin and, especially, the very durable Robert Loggia (an actor who not only gets better as the years pass but also, encouragingly, seems to be awarded with bigger and better parts). For all practical purposes Tony's world is

a man's world and the three women with anything other than
bit-parts and walk-ons do well to make their presence felt at
all. Miriam Colon did what she could with an underwritten
role – her displeasure with her son is never fully explained –
and Mary Elizabeth Mastrantonio manages to make her role
work despite the fact that she, too, has little to go on. Indeed,
both mother and daughter are popped on to the screen about
halfway through the film with hardly any indication before-
hand that they exist at all. The incest theme is more outspoken than in the 1932 film – Paul Muni merely looked fondly
at his sister, played by Ann Dvorak – but remains almost as
undeveloped.

The third woman, Michelle Pfeiffer, also suffers from a
thin role but commendably made the most of it. Discussing
the film with Peter Stone, for *Interview*, she remarked that
Elvira was 'a very cold and aloof woman – very different
from my personality and a difficult character for me to hold
on to'.

Pfeiffer was also obliged to display her talents through a
frozen shell, partly induced by the fact that her character was
permanently strung-out, and also through her make-up
which, she later commented, 'was always deathly white – for
six months I had to bleach my hair, wear fake nails, be
plastered in make-up and stay out of the sun.' The make-up,
face and body, took two hours to apply on each day of
shooting.

For all the inconveniences and the pressures of trying to
stay afloat in a sea of blood, bullets and foul language, she
was awarded with some good notices. *Variety* was sympa-
thetic, observing that she 'does well with a basically one-di-
mensional role'. Veteran film critic Richard Corliss, writing
in *Time* commented, 'Most of the large cast is fine: Michelle
Pfeiffer is better. [Her] Elvira is funny and pathetic, a street
angel ready at any whim to float away on another cocaine
cloud.'

She also had a couple of good lines. One, her exit line, was
delivered to Tony who clearly didn't understand her mean-

ing: 'Too bad we never grew up'. The other directly addressed an aspect of Stone's screenplay which caused almost as much criticism as did the visual violence. Tony Montana's English was not only learned from watching old gangster movies, he also picked up the four-letter word once banned in Hollywood but which now appears with monotonous regularity in everything from high drama to comedy. In its various forms and derivatives – used as noun, verb, adverb and adjective – the word 'fuck' is uttered, someone claims to have counted, 183 times. With perhaps conscious irony, Stone gave Elvira the line, 'Can't you stop saying "fuck" all the time?'.

The National Film Theatre notes, quoted earlier, observed that the original *Scarface* was vibrant 'with the impact of things that were real and deeply felt'.

Although no one can doubt the reality of drug-induced violence in Miami and, to be fair to this embattled city and the state of Florida, in many other parts of the USA and Europe, the after-effect of De Palma's *Scarface* is not one of deeply felt emotions. Rather, there is a sense of having watched an expensive and exceptionally well-made offering from New World Pictures' series of cheap exploitation films of the 1970s. And of disappointment that De Palma chose not to make his anti-drugs theme explicit.

There may have been a drug-induced ethereal quality about the character of Elvira, but it was nowhere near the other-worldliness of Pfeiffer's next role.

Directed by Richard Donner and filmed in Italy, *Ladyhawke* (1985) is a medieval myth which never fully escapes from its atmosphere of being a slightly juvenile sword-and-sorcery romp.

Some years ago, the Bishop of Aquila (John Wood) made advances to the beautiful Isabeau of Anjou (Pfeiffer) and when he was rejected petulantly placed a curse upon her and her lover, Etienne of Navarre (Rutger Hauer). Now, by day, Etienne appears in human form while she is a hawk; by night,

Isabeau resumes human form but he turns into a wolf. Thus, they are never apart but neither are they ever together.

Etienne is joined by a young pickpocket, Phillipe Gaston (Matthew Broderick), who cannot understand the frequent appearances and disappearances of the two lovers. When Isabeau is injured, Etienne and Phillipe set out to find Father Imperius (Leo McKern), who helped the bishop place the curse upon the couple, and who, Etienne believes, might now be able to save Isabeau's life.

Imperius helps the couple and, with Isabeau recovered, Etienne – helped by Phillipe, the only person ever to escape from the dungeons of Aquila – enters the fortified cathedral determined to end the bishop's malignant rule. After a sword fight, at the end of which Etienne defeats the bishop's Captain of the Guard, Marquet (Ken Hutchison), an eclipse of the sun allows the lovers a fleeting moment together. Then Etienne kills the bishop and the curse is lifted.

Pfeiffer was attracted to the film partly because, after *Scarface*, she was inundated with scripts in which her role would have been that of a coldly aloof bitch. In contrast, the *Ladyhawke* script struck her as being 'one of the most charming, sweet scripts I had ever read'.

In its manifestation, the screenplay, a collaboration by Edward Khmara, Michael Thomas and Tom Mankiewicz, is somewhat uneasy. Visually, it alternates between the dramatic expanses of a huge cathedral set and superb Italian (standing in for the script's French) locations, all masterfully photographed by Vittorio Storaro. The dialogue is much less satisfactory. Given the film's premise, neither of the two lovers has very much to say since only one of them can use a human voice at any one time. Most of the dialogue is therefore given to the top-billed Broderick, and it is an uneasy mixture of normal lines and internal monologues.

The love story element, which is essentially what this film is all about, is generally handled adroitly and so too are the action sequences. The decision to give the lead to Broderick, which thus emphasizes the juvenile aura with which the film is surrounded, means that he has too many scenes of some-what childish and not very funny comic intent. To some extent this failing is outweighed by Donner's crisp handling of the fight sequences and a surprisingly gentle touch he shows in the scenes in which Isabeau is in human form, alone in the forest save for her lupine companion. Donner had previously made the hugely successful *The Omen* (1976) and *Superman* (1978) and the Mel Gibson *Lethal Weapon* films.

Performances are variable. Wood's bishop doesn't have many moves other than to appear menacing; Hutchison, an old hand at Italian-made sword-and-cape epics, does well in a fairly narrow part; McKern rolls his sonorous voice across lines that are never as good as he makes them sound, or deserves, and is called upon from time to time to add a little weight to some of the supposedly comic scenes. Of the three leads, Broderick is clearly at sea. His earlier performance in *War Games* (1983) had been helped by an impressive display of computer hardware and assorted gimmickry; with only his acting ability to depend upon he is considerably less effective.

As Etienne, Rutger Hauer is mainly content to offer a brooding, black-clad presence akin to that he has adopted for several film roles, such as *The Hitcher* (1986) and the British television commercial for Guinness. He does what he does quite effectively, but there is not much flair to his perform-ance. As Isabeau, Michelle Pfeiffer had the same problems besetting her co-star, that of having to play all her most important scenes to a lover in non-human form, but she makes a better job of it. Despite some technical problems ('You can't help thinking, while you're dangling there, rigged up to a pulley, is this what I studied all those years for?'), Pfeiffer enjoyed making the film. In particular, she was thrilled by the trip to Europe, her first visit outside the USA. To while away the hours when she was not on the set or location she started painting, engrossing herself in technique and finding a necessary mental and psychological release.

And, also, a hobby which she continued after her return home.

The five-month-long trip also meant separation from her husband, Peter Horton; the first time this had happened for anything more than fleeting moments. Although she would state in interviews that her marriage was in good shape, the time in Italy placed stresses upon it which she energetically resolved to alleviate upon her return.

For all the failings of *Ladyhawke*, not least of which was its box-office results, which found little more than a third of its $21 million cost trickling back in, it did gain some good reviews and most concentrated upon Pfeiffer. Richard Corliss, in *Film Comment*, stated that she 'soars over the medieval silliness of Richard Donner's *Ladyhawke* like a princess high on her own mystery'. *Variety* remarked: 'Lovely Michelle Pfeiffer is perfect as the enchanting beauty . . .' Ann Lloyd, in *Films and Filming*, liked the film a lot: 'Ladyhawke would be a medieval fantasy, a sword and sorcery fable, if it were not first and foremost and overwhelmingly a love story. It's been a long time since such an unmolested love story was allowed to hit the screen.' This critic liked Pfeiffer even more, stating that she 'is a wonderful piece of casting. If a man of [Etienne] Navarre's standing and calibre is going to eat his heart out over a dame she has to be worth it, and this Lady Isabeau is a glorious example of the breathtakingly beautiful, and the noble and the covetable.'

Back in the USA, Pfeiffer embarked upon a television film directed by her husband. The film, which was made by Highgate Pictures and screened on the ABC network on 21 May 1985, after first being shown in the schools slot, was a twenty-minute dramatization of the dangers of teenage drinking habits. Entitled *One Too Many*, it starred Pfeiffer as a high-school student whose boyfriend, played by Val Kilmer (shortly to explode on the big screen as Jim Morrison in Oliver Stone's *The Doors*), is an alcoholic. Also featured in the film are Mare Winningham and Lance Guest. The film was praised and so too was Pfeiffer with John O'Connor in the *New York Times* declaring that she was 'powerfully affecting'.

Shortly before *One Too Many*, Pfeiffer also helped set up a television production company with Horton and his career continued to develop as writer and director but would not take off fully until he was cast as Gary in the television drama series *thirtysomething*.

In the meantime, Pfeiffer was cast for the first time in a comedy role. This was in director John Landis's *Into the Night* (1985) in which she plays the role of a disaster-prone young woman who has unwisely, not to say illegally, smuggled precious stones into the country.

A bored executive, Ed Okin (Jeff Goldblum), discovers that his wife, Ellen (Stacey Picken), is unfaithful. If his boring job and his shattered homelife were not enough for any man to suffer, Ed is also an insomniac. With his wife's infidelity preying on his mind, he climbs into his car and drifts sleeplessly through Los Angeles, ending up at the airport where he meets Diana (Pfeiffer) who is being pursued by a group of murderous Iranians, the Savaks. Diana scrambles into Ed's car and he takes her to her brother, Charlie (Bruce McGill, who had worked with Pfeiffer on the television series *Delta House*). Charlie is not at all happy to see them and refuses to help his flaky sister. Diana decides instead to seek the help of her friend Christie (Kathryn Harrold) but, before they can leave, Ed's car is towed away. Undeterred, Diana steals Charlie's car – even though this is a highly identifiable white convertible, ostensibly once the property of Elvis Presley, which Charlie, an Elvis buff, values greatly.

Christie is an actress in television series, *Kalijak*, and Ed and Diana head for the studios where she is working. Diana asks Christie to keep something for her and only later tells Ed that she has smuggled into the country some emeralds, once the property of the Shah of Iran, which the Savaks want to recover at all costs. Diana believes that the people for whom she smuggled the jewels will help her but they are all found murdered. Diana is taken prisoner by hitman Colin

Morris (David Bowie), who works for Monsieur Melville (Roger Vadim) who is also determined to have the emeralds.

Ed helps Diana escape and she now tries to engage the help of reclusive millionaire Jack Caper (Richard Farnsworth). She was once Caper's mistress but he will no longer have anything to do with her. With nowhere left to turn, Ed and Diana return to Charlie's but Melville and his men are there waiting. Ed and Diana are taken to Christie's home to collect the emeralds but when they arrive the actress has been murdered by the Savaks. Despite the presence of the police, Diana casually picks up Christie's coat, knowing that there is a secret pocket in which the actress has hidden the jewels.

By now, Ed is desperately tired but still incapable of sleep. He and Diana return to Caper, insist on seeing him and secure his help. He tells them that the Savaks are in the employment of Shaheen Parvizi (Irene Papas) and that their only hope is to offer to sell the emeralds to her with assurances that they will be left unharmed.

Ed and Diana evolve a scheme and manage to escape to the airport with the money they have been given by Parvizi but their flight to Mexico is delayed and a gun battle erupts between the Savaks and the FBI. Diana is captured by one of the Savaks who threatens to kill her but when he sees that his position is hopeless he shoots himself.

Ed and Diana receive a suitcase filled with money from Jack Caper, whose involvement is deeper than he has allowed, and at a motel Ed is finally able to sleep. When he awakens Diana has gone, taking the suitcase but leaving behind some of the money. He sets out to search for her but finally gives up, believing that she has gone from his life forever. But then she reappears, still carrying the suitcase.

For all its complexities of plot, director Landis carries off the film with considerable élan, all the more remarkable because at the time of its making he was waiting to go on trial for his involvement in the accidental deaths of actor Vic Morrow and two young Asian children during the filming of Landis's segment of the 1982 portmanteau film, *The Twilight Zone*. Charged with four others, Landis faced several years in prison and very heavy fines and damages if found guilty of involuntary manslaughter. Two years later, in May 1987, Landis and his co-defendants were acquitted.

Landis has a penchant for irreverent comedy; apart from *National Lampoon's Animal House* he also directed *Kentucky Fried Movie* (1977), *The Blues Brothers* (1980) and two Eddie Murphy vehicles, *Trading Places* (1983) and *Coming to America* (1988). He also demonstrated great visual flair with the rock video, *Michael Jackson's Thriller*.

Ron Koslow's screenplay for *Into the Night* is filled with film industry in-jokes and there are enough famous faces (or, at least, famous names) wandering through in small roles, bit parts and walk-ons to keep film buffs entertained even if the film itself was not worth watching – which it always is. Apart from names already mentioned are actors, writers, directors and others such as Dan Aykroyd, David Cronenberg, Waldo Salt, Daniel Petrie, Paul Mazursky, Jonathan Lynn, Don Siegel, Robert Paynter (the film's cinematographer), Lawrence Kasdan, Vera Miles, Clu Gulager, Paul Bartel, Jonathan Demme, and Jon Stephen Fink. Landis himself also plays a small part and so, too, does DeeDee Pfeiffer. Following her sister into films, DeeDee's career has been inevitably overshadowed but she has worked steadily if unspectacularly, appearing in, amongst others, *The Midnight Hour, Toughlove* (both 1985), *The Allnighter* (1987) and *Brothers in Arms* (1989).

The hectic pace of *Into the Night* and the fun generated are not the only striking qualities; what makes it more than just another caper movie is Landis's willingness to shadow the comedy with what is often quite graphic violence. The manner in which the man who holds Diana hostage at the airport kills himself, putting his gun into his mouth, pulling the trigger and spattering blood and brains over Diana and Ed, shows a measure of confidence few comic-caper directors would normally risk.

And the significance of all the murderous events is not lost on Ed who, virtually sleepwalking though he might be, continually discovers that everything he (and through him the audience) fears about life in the city is not only true but often nightmarishly worse than he imagined. Jeff Goldblum usually has a wild-eyed intensity that allows him to enter into comic or dramatic roles with equal flair. Here, his eyes are anything but wild and wide and his deliberately sleepy performance forms a solid centre around which most of the zany and freewheeling comedy frantically spins.

Also frantically spinning is the effervescent Diana and Pfeiffer's performance was remarked upon in *Variety*. 'Thanks to a perfect portrayal by Michelle Pfeiffer, there's a pleasantly painful memory or two here for any man who has ever ventured near one of those beautiful wackos who are nothing but trouble but impossible to resist. Make no mistake: this is not a Goldie Hawn sweet thing with a streak of bad luck. Pfeiffer's inspiration is major-league, top-of-the-line, state-of-the-art Bimboism in full bloom, the kind whose clothes are stored from one end of LA to the other, along with whatever morals she might have hit town with originally.'

Certainly, Pfeiffer takes to comedy with considerable flair, displaying confidence and excellent timing and somehow making the wild-at-heart character of Diana seem wholly probable. Her confidence was remarked upon by Bruce McGill who said that since he had last worked with her, in 1979, she had changed for the better. 'Without being a prima donna, she now has as much faith in her opinion of a scene as in anyone else's.'

Although Pfeiffer has made comments which would contradict this: 'I have five opinions about everything,' there is an undoubted maturity in her work on *Into the Night*. While she makes the zaniness of her character entirely believable, there is never any doubt that underlying Diana's pin-ball ricocheting from one crisis to another is a woman who will survive.

The ability to imbue her character with these apparently

conflicting traits without revealing the craftswoman at work beneath is something few actresses of her age and experience could accomplish. Harlow, perhaps, from the past; no one from the present.

Richard Corliss, in *Film Comment*, happily linked Pfeiffer's name not only with Harlow but also with some other great names from Hollywood's past. 'She is Jean Harlow who taught herself to be Carole Lombard; and she is displaying, in John Landis's *Into the Night*, a laser-light comic touch reminiscent of both these stars. She is Marilyn Monroe carrying off a masquerade as Grace Kelly . . .'

Heady company, indeed, but very largely justified. Perhaps helped by the variety of her last three roles, Pfeiffer found herself not only a star but also seriously regarded as an actress with a great deal to offer and with, so far, no apparent limitations. The frozen, cocaine-addicted beauty of Elvira lingered in memories despite all the gory mayhem around her in *Scarface*. A different kind of translucent beauty had illumined *Ladyhawke*. And now, with *Into the Night*, she had proved that she could not only act comedy but could also carry an entire film with seemingly effortless ease.

She was well-poised to take on pretty nearly anything, provided she received the right kind of offers. Still a few years away from being able to develop her own projects, she was already at risk of being spoiled for choice; but, for the most part, she chose well. If, in a sense, her next three films marked time, none of them did her any harm while an appearance in a television drama gave her a role which carried with it innumerable echoes of the kind of problem many beautiful screen actresses of the past, and present, found hard to handle.

4   *Manipulation, Mystique and Magic*

Michelle Pfeiffer's newly discovered ability to play comedy convincingly was employed next in a delightful dual role in Alan Alda's *Sweet Liberty* (1985).

Alda established his reputation as an actor, and occasional writer and director, in the long-running television series, *M*A*S*H*. The show clocked up an astonishing 251 episodes and a truly remarkable audience for the final two-hour episode, in 1983, which was variously estimated at between 85 and 125 million viewers. During the show's eleven-year run, numerous Emmy Awards came its way including three for Alda, in 1974, 1977 and 1981–2. On the big screen Alda appeared in a small number of films during the 1960s and '70s including *Same Time, Next Year* (1978), *The Seduction of Joe Tynan* (1979), for which he also wrote the screenplay, and *The Four Seasons* (1981), also writing and directing.

Sweet Liberty found Alda again wearing three hats, as writer, director and leading man. Alda plays the role of Michael Burgess, a history teacher in Sayeville, a small town in North Carolina, who has recently enjoyed unexpected success as an author. Now his book, *Sweet Liberty*, an academic study of the War of Independence, is to be made into a film.

The arrival in town of a Hollywood film crew turns Sayeville on its ear. At first Michael is excitedly co-operating with the film's director, Bo Hodges (Saul Rubinek), and writer, Stanley Gould (Bob Hoskins), but his enthusiasm is heightened when he meets the actors, especially Faith Healey (Pfeiffer), who is to play the role of Mary Slocombe, a real-life heroine of the war against the British. Caught up in preparations for filming, Michael is encouraged to find that Stanley is in awe of him. The screenwriter constantly tells Michael how much he envies his being a real writer and not a mere Hollywood hack. Michael is even more flattered when Faith forms what appears to be a warm friendship with him and insists that he should help her with her interpretation of her role.

Michael's pleasure is at first lightly punctured by differences with his girlfriend, Gretchen Carlson (Lise Hilboldt), who has been trying unsuccessfully to persuade Michael into marriage. He likes their relationship as it is; intimate but separate and with no ties that would seriously bind him. Not surprisingly, Gretchen disapproves of his friendship with Faith and warns him that this will damage their own relationship.

Michael doesn't take any of this too seriously and is, anyway, completely immersed in the making of the film. But his delight in events, and his illusions, are soon shattered. The film Hodges plans to make is nothing like the accurate slice of history recounted in Michael's studious book. The director has his eye fixed firmly on the box-office, declaring that to succeed in this business 'you make movies for a young market, and you have only to think of three things. One, defy authority; two, destroy property; three, take people's clothes off.'

As Hodges proceeds to do just this, aided by the amiable hack writer, Stanley, Michael finds that even Faith is not what she seems. When she is acting the role of Mary Slocombe, Faith is a picture of wan innocence and fragility; as herself, she is hard-bitten, self-centred, and will use anyone and any means to advance her career. Even her encouragement of Michael to help her with her lines is part of her determined self-advancement. In her hotel room, he hears her on the telephone cursing furiously at her agent. Shocked, he tells her, 'You're two different people.' 'If I could only be two people,' she snaps back, 'I'd be out of business.'

If all this were not enough for the growingly disillusioned Michael, he discovers that the romance he thought was blossoming between himself and Faith is not only designed to keep him as an ally in the advancement of her career but is also just one of her ongoing affairs. She is also enjoying a closer-than-close working relationship with her co-star of the film, Elliott James (Michael Caine), who is playing the role of Colonel Tarleton, commander of the British Green Dragoons.

Michael, encouraged verbally but not in reality, by Stanley, attempts to drag the film back into the realms of historical accuracy but the director will have none of it. Even the Green Dragoons' distinctive green uniforms are changed to red because this colour will look better on the screen.

At first irritated by Elliott, Michael slowly forms an uneasy relationship with him but only after the actor defeats him at fencing, a skill the actor has developed during a career in sword-and-cape adventures. But the casual manner in which the actors drift into and out of relationships becomes steadily more difficult for Michael to handle. His brief fling with Faith is quickly forgotten by the actress as she drifts into an 'on-location' affair with Elliott. But Elliott, veteran swordsman in bed as well as out, is harassed by the unexpected arrival in Sayeville of his wife, Leslie (Lois Chiles).

Michael's problems are not helped by Gretchen's employment on the film as Faith's needlework teacher. Nevertheless, his relationship with Gretchen is healed by their attempts to ease the distress of his ailing mother, Cecelia (Lillian Gish), who, from her hospital bed, attempts to maintain her years-long obsession with a former boyfriend, Johnny Delvechio (Richard Whiting). But when Michael eventually locates his mother's old flame he finds that he has been married for more than forty years.

As filming reaches its end and director Hodges prepares to shoot the climactic battle scene, Michael's barely suppressed anger with what is being done to his book and, worse, to history, finally erupts. Hired as an extra for the battle, along with a host of local historical war games enthusiasts, he decides to change the course of the film, rather than let the film change the course of history. Knowing that whatever happens during the battle, the film company will be unable to afford the time or the money to reshoot the sequence, he plots with his fellow 'revolutionaries' and instead of fleeing the battlefield before the British guns, which is what Hodges wants, they charge them. Hodges, pragmatic if nothing else, knows a good action sequence when he sees one and keeps his cameras running.

The film completed, the crew packs up to leave and makes its cheerful farewells seemingly unaware that their presence has changed many things about Sayeville, not least the lives of some of the town's inhabitants.

With things getting back to as near normal as is possible, Michael agrees that he and Gretchen should live together in a trial marriage. Several months later, when the film is given its world premiere in Sayeville, and is clearly heading for box-office success, Gretchen is pregnant and Michael is happy at last.

As Alda has revealed in some of his earlier work, especially his elegiac treatment of *The Four Seasons*, a film which charts with perception, wit and empathy, the development of personal relationships between middle-aged, middle-Americans, he hankers after a past when unpleasant things, such as duplicity, guile, boorishness, crassness and outrageous vulgarity did not exist. Well, of course they existed, but have faded into oblivion thanks to the soothing effect of nostalgia. In some ways, the undertow of *Sweet Liberty*, which contrasts small-town values with unprincipled Hollywood, allows Alda to once again state his case, of which he appears surprisingly certain.

Somewhat less certain is the attitude expressed by Alda's character in the film. In the early moments of *Sweet Liberty* Michael is much too trusting. True, there are university professors and high-school teachers whose grasp of real-world values and attitudes is tenuous to say the least, but Alda's playing of the role makes him initially too worldly, too modern, too *smart*, to make credible his later shift through disbelief to frustrated anger. James Stewart might have made it work, via Frank Capra, but Alda via Alda doesn't. Or maybe it's just echoes of *M*A*S*H*'s 'Hawkeye' Pierce who, for all his occasional lapses into sentimentality, never let anybody put one over on him.

Bob Hoskins, all bright-eyed eagerness and barely concealed vulgarity, as the untalented screenwriter, expertly conveys the conflict of emotions present in a man who, deep down, knows that he hasn't a fraction of the history teacher's intellectual capacity or his skill as a writer, but earns ten times as much churning out pot-boiling scripts for cheapskate movies. In Hoskins's hands Stanley Gould is as cheap, loud and potentially threadbare as the shirts he wears. Curiously enough for someone who, as himself, sounds the very epitome of the tough-talking Londoner, Hoskins has found himself playing a surprising number of Americans. He does so with considerable flair, usually managing, as he does here, to look the part as well.

Saul Rubinek enjoys his role as the director of the film within the film and he, too, dresses the part; in his case as the would-be-with-it hipster who is already fast-approaching the sell-by date for would-be brat-packers. On the whole, however, the film-crew roles are not as well written, or even depicted, as those in the film-within-the-film created by Jack Rosenthal for his British television play, *Ready When You Are, Mr McGill*.

As the ageing swordsman, Michael Caine also appears to enjoy his role and for once his customary deadpan, flat-voiced characterization works quite well. Indeed, there is more than a hint that Caine is playing the role as if it is himself; at least himself as others might see him.

Some of the other roles, especially those played by Lise Hilboldt and Lillian Gish, appear almost afterthoughts and leave them too little to do but struggle to make an impact with underwritten parts.

As the sweet-faced heroine of the War of Independence,

Pfeiffer manages just the right touch of strong-minded inno-cence. As the foul-mouthed conniving and manipulative Hollywood star she is so real that speculation surfaces as to who she is modelling her role upon; except, of course, it could be almost anyone. The deceptively casual ease with which she slips from role to role with no more than eye-blink hesitation shows that the comic potential revealed in *Into the Night* was no fluke.

She received some good reviews, including *Films and Film-ing*'s Audrey Smith who referred to 'the delectable cameo of the film's leading lady (American Revolution style) from the lovely Michelle Pfeiffer.'

In the long term, however, the most important aspect of Pfeiffer's stint in the Hamptons on Long Island, where *Sweet Liberty* was shot, was her meeting with Kate Guinzburg, the film's production office co-ordinator. They struck up a friendship and discovered that they held similar views about the industry in which they were working. A few years later, this relationship blossomed into Pfeiffer-Guinzburg Produc-tions, a company which would oversee the actress's move into a position of power in Hollywood.

On the surface, Pfeiffer's decision to appear in a tiny role in *Amazon Women on the Moon* (1986) seems not merely odd but a retrogressive move in her burgeoning career. The film is a scatter-gun collection of twenty-odd comedy sketches, some of which hit their target while others miss the mark by a mile. In fact, her appearance was influenced by two factors. *Amazon Women on the Moon* was masterminded by John Landis with whom she had worked so successfully on *Into the Night* and Pfeiffer's husband, Peter Horton, was to direct one of the sketches and was also to act with her in another. The chance to work with Horton had a sub-text. Although the couple were still on very good terms, their marriage was in trouble and working together on a project, even one as disjointed as this, at least gave them a feeling of togetherness.

Among the film's sketches, the one which provides the overall title is a very good spoof of a 1950s low-budget sci-fi movie. The sketch stars Steve Forrest as an astronaut who lands on a world inhabited entirely by women. Another good sketch features Ed Begley Jnr as a harmless lunatic who believes he is the son of the Invisible Man and who periodically takes off his clothes and runs around naked imagining that no one can see him. Because his friends and acquaintances know and like him, they play along with his fantasy. An almost-there sketch proposed the idea of a black entertainer, Don 'No Soul' Simmons (David Alan Grier), who performs in the bland manner of Liberace.

In a sketch set in the maternity ward of a large hospital a crazed obstetrician (Griffin Dunne) tries to conceal the fact that the staff has lost a new-born baby. When the upwardly-mobile, childbirth-experience-sharing parents, Brenda and Harry (Pfeiffer and Horton), become steadily more panic-stricken, the doctor placates them with various ploys including trying to pass off a Mr Potato Head toy as their missing child. This sketch is one of the film's near-misses and so, too, is one, directed by Horton, which features Rosanne Arquette and Steve Guttenberg as two blind-daters.

Unfortunately, the misses outweigh the hits and perhaps Landis's decision to share direction with Horton, Joe Dante, Robert K. Weiss and Carl Gottlieb compounded the uncertainties and unevenness. In the event, *Amazon Women on the Moon* drifted into the obscurity of late-night television.

Despite the fact that Pfeiffer and Horton were working together and maintaining cordial relations, their marriage continued to deteriorate. But they persisted with the relationship because, as Horton would later state, they still loved one another. Increasingly, however, they were recognizing that love was not enough.

During the period when their marital problems were reaching crisis-point, Pfeiffer agreed to take the lead in a television drama and a new film, working on them simultaneously. Her performance in the film, which gave her yet another comedy role, this time as the widow of a mafia hitman, offered no hint of her personal state of mind, such was her professionalism. The television drama cut much closer to the bone, reflecting in some measure the emotional problems she was currently enduring in her marriage.

Natica Jackson (1987) was part of a television series entitled *Tales from the Hollywood Hills,* made for transmission on the PBS channel in the USA and also co-funded by Channel 4 who screened it in Britain.

Pfeiffer takes the title role, that of a Hollywood actress in the 1930s whose career is starting to blossom. While she and her agents, Morris and Ernestine King (Hector Elizondo and Holland Taylor), negotiate a new contract with the studio boss, Brad Loring (George Murdock), Natica cannot overcome her growing disillusionment at the isolation stardom brings.

Her need for someone in her life with whom she can have an unforced, loving relationship bursts through when she has a minor accident while driving her car. The other driver involved is Hal Graham (Brian Kerwin), a chemist with Signal Oil. He is married with two children; an ordinary, decent man who is not in the least in awe of her stardom. For the first time, Natica can drop the veil of pretence which clouds her life and begin to live and love like other people – like she might have done had she remained plain Anna Jacobs.

Inevitably, however, their love affair begins to affect Natica's work and it also affects Hal, whose wife, Beryl (Gail Youngs), suspects her husband's infidelity. Despite the efforts of Natica's friends and colleagues, she ignores their advice. She also ignores threats from her employers. Hollywood studios of the 1930s did, of course, have so-called 'morals clauses' written into stars' contracts in the hope of preventing adultery and other stumbles from the straight and narrow path of propriety. Despite the term given to the clause, the studios were not morally outraged by such activities; they simply didn't want any bad publicity. However, Natica clings on to Hal but then Beryl Graham, pregnant with her third child, cracks under the strain and drowns her other two children.

Emotionally shattered by this terrible outcome of her affair with Hal, Natica knows that from here on, for the rest of her life, her movie-star mystique will come between her and men and that she is doomed to endure a life of loneliness, brightened only briefly and dimly by unfulfilling affairs. Portentously, Natica's latest film, which will seal her stardom, is entitled *Dark Voyage*.

Throughout, the production shows a deep understanding of the attitudes and behaviour of the times in which *Natica Jackson* is set. Everything about it looks good and even the slightly hazy quality of the photography and subdued colour helps to create an atmosphere redolent of the era.

Although the manner in which the two lovers find one another smacks rather of old-style Hollywood 'meeting cute', the darkness which descends upon Natica and Hal cleaves to the heart of the kind of emotional problem many people in the public eye must suffer in part-payment for their fame.

Pfeiffer's performance is excellent, readily creating the impression of a major star-in-the-making; which, indeed, is what she was herself at this point in her career. All the supporting cast do well, with Kerwin finding the right balance of mixed emotions for man caught between pleasantly undemanding domestic stability and the fire of a once-in-a-lifetime passion.

Pfeiffer was variously reported as having based her characterization upon 1930s Hollywood stars such as Katharine Hepburn, Norma Shearer and Carole Lombard, although it is hard to see such reflections in her interpretation, at least insofar as Hepburn and Shearer are concerned. In any event, it was not merely a good performance in a good television film, it was also a measure of the actress's desire to take roles with depth even if the money, and the exposure, were much less than she could now expect.

Director Paul Bogart remarked that Pfeiffer had 'identified

very strongly with Natica who could be bartered and exchanged like a piece of merchandise. Michelle felt she understood what it was like to be a kind of commodity.'

Bogart himself has worked extensively in television, winning Emmy Awards for *The Defenders, Dear Friends, Shadow Game* and *All in the Family*. His film credits include *Marlowe* (1969) and *Skin Game* (1971).

The film Pfeiffer had worked on while making *Natica Jackson* was not yet ready for release. In the meantime, she took fourth billing in what was, in career terms, her most important film to date.

Michael Cristofer based his screenplay for *The Witches of Eastwick* (1987) upon John Updike's novel. In both Cristofer's concept and director George Miller's realization of the project, certain decisions were made which altered the thrust of the story. To a great extent, Updike used witchcraft metaphorically in pursuit of the meaning of love and the nature of physical attraction between the sexes. A recurring theme in Updike's work, also present here, is his exploration of the manners, morals and mores of small-town America. Witchcraft – spells, rituals, magic, demons – gave Updike the material with which to weave his tapestry; Cristofer and Miller chose to concentrate upon the threads themselves and somewhere along the way allowed the bigger picture to fade into a pale facsimile of the novelist's intent.

This is not in itself necessarily a negative criticism; screenplays based upon novels must make changes. Indeed, a case might be mounted to support the view that adaptations that fail do so because they haven't changed the novel enough. When an idea for a story is conceived, the author decides in what form he will develop it. If he decides upon a novel he will treat his idea in a certain manner; if he decides upon a screenplay he will choose a different treatment. It might therefore be argued that the best way to approach an adaptation is to largely ignore the form of the novel and instead go back to the novelist's original conception and redevelop the treatment along filmic lines.

In the event, the film version of *The Witches of Eastwick* treats Updike's deep and complex ideas as the basis for a kind of amalgam of *Carrie, Three Bad Sisters* and *The Exorcist* with little bits of *Ghostbusters* thrown in for good measure.

In the film, three women friends live in the small New England town of Eastwick. Outwardly, they are fairly normal; but each possesses supernatural powers. Alexandra Medford (Cher), a widow, is a sculptor who makes small figurines of females, vaguely fertility symbols, which she supplies to a local souvenir store. Highly intelligent, Alex despairs of a life that is empty of the kind of intellectual and sexual stimulation she needs. Jane Spofford (Susan Sarandon) is divorced and similarly unattached. A cellist, she teaches music but cannot bring to her own playing the passionate intensity needed for a professional career. As a result she is angrily frustrated in both her musical and domestic life. Sukie Ridgemont (Pfeiffer), although in some ways immature and childlike, is an abandoned mother of six (her children include one set each of triplets and twins). She is a reporter on a local newspaper; ideally, Sukie would be an investigative journalist but her editor wants only a quiet life and, anyway, nothing scandalous ever happens in Eastwick.

The three women idle away some time conjuring up an ideal lover, not realizing the strength of their strange powers. A short time later they learn that one of Eastwick's biggest houses, the empty Lenox mansion, has been bought by a stranger, Daryl Van Horne (Jack Nicholson). Some of the conservationist (and very conservative-minded) townspeople worry over the fact that the grounds of the Lenox mansion are home to snowy egrets and Felicia Alden (Veronica Cartwright) is particularly outspoken against the newcomer. Felicia's objections are interrupted when she suffers a mysterious accident, perhaps the result of a spell.

Then the newcomer meets Alex, buys up all her figurines, her 'bubbies' as she calls them, takes her to his mansion for lunch, and seduces her. Van Horne also convinces Alex of the truth of something she already senses, that she is meant

Greasers' delight:
'Stephanie' dreams of bikers'
heaven in *Grease 2*

A joint hot property that didn't quite catch fire: 'Stephanie' and
Maxwell Caulfield in *Grease 2*

Slightly stoned: 'Elvira'
drifting on a cloud of coke in
Scarface

Out of the forest: the enchanted 'Isabeau' in *Ladyhawke*

Grace under pressure: suffering nobly as 'Isabeau' in
Ladyhawke

Please, I need my zees: insomniac 'Ed' and wide-awake 'Diana'
in *Into the Night* with Jeff Goldblum

A wrong number: accident-
prone 'Diana' in *Into the
Night*

Don't knock: the manipulatively innocent 'Faith'/'Mary' in *Sweet Liberty*

Bubble, bubble: spellbindingly childlike 'Sukie' in *The Witches of Eastwick* with Susan Sarandon (*centre*) and Cher (*right*)

An offer she can refuse: newly widowed 'Angela' pursued by Dean Stockwell in *Married to the Mob*

Heading for a hiding place: 'Angela', the brand-new you, in *Married to the Mob*

Dish of the day: 'Jo Ann' and Kurt Russell, two sides of an unequal triangle in *Tequila Sunrise*

Fair game: 'Madame de Tourvel' and her would-be seducer in *Dangerous Liaisons* with John Malkovich

Hot piano: 'Susie' makin' whoopee with Jeff Bridges in *The Fabulous Baker Boys*

Torch Song: 'Susie' the sizzling chanteuse in *The Fabulous Baker Boys*

for better things. He persuades her to extend her craft by sculpting bigger and better bubbies and setting up a deal with a New York retail outlet. Van Horne then calls upon the music teacher and joins her in a ferocious cello duet that is more sexual than musical. Jane's long-suppressed passionate nature is finally released and she becomes his second, and this time resident, lover. When Alex introduces Sukie to Van Horne, the three friends become rivals for the stranger's affections, or at least for a share of his sexual prowess.

Having moved in to the mansion, where all four are waited upon by Van Horne's manservant, Fidel (Carel Struycken), they find themselves the target of Eastwick's scandalized residents. Felicia Alden becomes steadily more virulent to the point where she begins vomiting vast amounts of bile. This so outrages her peaceable husband, newspaper editor Clyde Alden (Richard Jenkins), that he kills her.

When Alex, Jane and Sukie learn of this they realize that things have gone too far and determine to leave Van Horne. But they have now become his pawns and, what's more, all three are pregnant by him. Knowing that they invoked Van Horne, they believe that they can make him leave and thus gain their release. They make an effigy of him, torturing it in their efforts to rid themselves of this awful demon. Now Van Horne reveals himself in all his frightening demonic majesty and attacks the mansion where the three women cower in fear. They manage to destroy the effigy and Van Horne vanishes.

The three women remain in the mansion during their pregnancies, served by Fidel, and thereafter guard their new-born children against their devilish father who plaintively appears before them all by way of multiple video screens.

As the leading actor in the film, Nicholson makes sure that his is the performance audiences will remember; a performance not a million miles removed from that he gave seven years earlier when he went completely over the top in *The Shining*. Of course, one must imagine that if the Devil were to take on human form he wouldn't look quite like the man next door; but then, he is hardly likely to appear wearing Nicholson's patented all-purpose devilish grin and a tasteless wardrobe apparently left over from a Roger Corman cheap-o horror flick (and designed for someone about a foot taller).

With a bravura performance from the star, the three leading ladies have an uphill struggle from the start if they are to make an impact. Susan Sarandon must have been the most discomfited; apparently cast as Alex, on the eve of filming she discovered that, as a result of disagreements between the director and the producer, Cher had been given that role and instead Sarandon was to play the somewhat ill-defined role of Jane. To make matters worse, she was faced, virtually overnight, with having to learn enough about the cello to make a reasonable stab at correct bowing and fingering (she was coached by Virginia Burward-Hoy). For all the problems with which she was beset, Sarandon does well with the role, effectively conveying the improbable unleashing of her sexuality during her dazzling and devilishly difficult duet with Nicholson.

The role of Alex, the most overtly sexual of the three women, is well-suited to Cher's stage persona although in her film roles she has made commendable strides in recreating herself in different images. Her success in making such changes in herself had apparently not reached the ears of director George Miller who made it abundantly clear to anyone who cared to listen that casting Cher in the film was not his idea. For all such difficulties, however, Cher easily becomes the most dominant of the three, which is what Alex is supposed to be.

As the whey-faced, excessively fecund Sukie, Pfeiffer contrives to look the part of the easily-ruled, weak-willed, ever-hopeful reporter who is horrified to discover that she becomes not the investigator but the subject of a story fit for the most outrageous scandal sheet. Sukie's childlike simplicity which sits in total contrast with her Earth Mother demeanour, is something Pfeiffer conveys with great skill. And even the fact that she is punished by the demon with the infliction of a rash of weeping facial sores does not entirely disfigure her.

Like Sarandon, Pfeiffer was also caught in the crossfire between director and producer and had to read for the part although Miller had already made it clear he wanted her. Reading or testing is not something she objects to doing; as she told Peter Stone in *Interview*, 'You know, I'm not really that proud – I'll go in and read; I'll go in and test. If I really want to do something, I'll go in and do whatever the director feels that he needs me to do.'

At various moments in the film the characterizations each of the stars has developed mesh comfortably with one another but too often there is a mild disorientation as if one or the other of them has inadvertently wandered in from an adjoining set housing an entirely different film.

Of the other actors in the film only a few have an opportunity to show what they can do; notably Veronica Cartwright, before she is killed off, and Carel Struycken, whose deadpan performance nicely offsets Nicholson's histrionics. Indeed, Struycken's appearance – black-clad, sombre mien, death's-head make-up – is considerably like how most people imagine, or fear, the devil to be. (Struycken also contributed the song, 'Peodora', to the soundtrack.)

Although the special effects are all done well, not all are really right for the film. The scene in which Van Horne and his harem release themselves from earthly constraints and 'fly' over the swimming pool doesn't have much to do with anything that is happening in the storyline. On the other hand, Van Horne's struggle to walk along Eastwick's main street against a hurricane-force wind spirited up by the three women is pertinent. Unfortunately, somewhat disconcertingly, it looks a little like a dark-side-of-the-coin version of Buster Keaton's similar struggle as Steamboat Bill Jnr.

Significantly at odds with the story – at least Updike's conception – is the understated motivation of the three women to, first, involve themselves with the Devil, and, second, to shift from eager collaboration with him to plotting his destruction.

In Updike's tale, the three are seeking fulfilment as women. The author is also deeply interested in how most dreams of love and happiness, understanding and personal achievement, are doomed, it would seem inevitably, to disintegration through the passage of time. Nothing lasts, not friendships, not promises, not beliefs, and certainly not sexual relationships whether founded in love or lust. In the film version, the three seem to be eager only for the relief of boredom.

The trio's decision to rid themselves of Van Horne is, in the film, little more than an awkward and only part-way reversion to middle-American morality. In the novel, the three revenge themselves upon Van Horne chiefly because he seduces and marries Jenny, the daughter of Clyde and Felicia Alden. Until this point, the three had looked on Jenny with a kind of nostalgic affection, seeing her, through rosecoloured glasses or not, as themselves when still young, innocent and untroubled by the world and still filled with hopes, ambitions and belief in the power of love. Jenny's relationship with Van Horne so angers them that they deliberately destroy her before driving him off. The character of Jenny – and hence this entire area of interesting psychological exploration – is omitted from the screenplay.

John Updike, author of the original novel, was not too happy with the result. 'I couldn't make myself read the script at all,' he said, but added that he did see the finished film and recognized 'echoes of my own dialogue'.

Reviews of *The Witches of Eastwick* were mixed; indeed, some were polarized. *Variety* saw it as brilliantly conceived metaphor for the battle of the sexes while Martin Sutton, in *Films and Filming*, was much less enamoured of the changes made to the novel, declaring that, 'Ultimately, however, the amiable skylarking cannot cover up the fact that what has been done to Updike's drama results in a movie which shoots off uneasily in all directions at once.'

For all its flaws, however, *The Witches of Eastwick* was not only a big-budget, star-studded extravaganza, it was also a box-office hit and these factors more than outweighed Pfeiffer's fourth-billing. In Hollywood's terms she had come of age. From here on, the kind of script to come her way was raised several notches and she would benefit enormously from this shift. The benefits would be not only in terms of quality but also variety. Film-makers were starting to realize that beneath the flawless-skinned, sweetness and light exterior, lay the complex heart and soul of a real actress.

On a personal level, the film was also immensely valuable because it brought Pfeiffer into close contact with two major stars and cult-figures (Cher and Nicholson) and an actress of immense depths and talent (Sarandon). Studying them at work helped refine her own growing knowledge of her craft. Additionally, she formed warm friendships with all three, that with Cher being especially close and lasting although it took some time to break through natural reserve. As Cher said, 'Michelle is very difficult to know. . . She has to know that she can trust you and you have to really go through a whole lot of stuff first.'

New and changing personal relationships were not the only important things happening in Pfeiffer's life at this time. Amongst the next films to be released was the one from which she had taken brief leave to make *Natica Jackson* for television, and another in which she would display a hitherto hidden talent for singing (*Grease 2* notwithstanding).

There would also be recognition of her talent from her peers: her first nominations for the annual awards made by the Academy of Motion Picture Arts and Sciences – the Oscars.

5   *Fabulous Liaisons*

As she approached the age of thirty, Michelle Pfeiffer began making changes; some personal, other professional, and all with far-reaching effects upon her life and career.

Her marriage to Peter Horton was at a very low ebb although they still enjoyed one another's company. They would remain friends but both could now acknowledge that they had changed since 1981 and that while friendship was still possible, even desirable, marriage was not. Their separation began during the period when Pfeiffer was working back-to-back on *Natica Jackson* and *Married to the Mob*, the emotional demands and pressures of her work helping submerge, if not drown out completely, her personal difficulties.

Not long after this decision was reached she was widely reported to have formed a close relationship with actor Michael Keaton (who would take the title role in the 1989 film, *Batman*). Their affair was intense and would end only when she was plunged unexpectedly into a searing and emotionally damaging relationship with another actor, a married man she would meet while filming in Europe.

Despite her demanding work schedule and her intense personal relationships, Pfeiffer was also anxious at this time to redress her failure to develop her education while at Fountain Valley High School. Eager to make up for the time she had spent on the beach when she should have been studying, she and her friend and business partner, Kate Guinzburg, decided to attend a course in medieval philosophy at the University of California at Los Angeles. Guinzburg would comment on Pfeiffer's compulsion for self-improvement and voracious appetite for reading; an appetite that was almost indiscriminate so wide was its range.

Pfeiffer was also keen to infuse her film roles with as much accurate detail as possible and she spent many hours working on her accent for her role as a mafia hitman's soon-to-be-widowed wife.

Married to the Mob (1988) is a freewheeling, occasionally anarchic and always studiously observed comedy. Directed by Jonathan Demme from a screenplay by Barry Strugatz and Mark R. Burns, the film centres upon the behaviour of the growingly dissatisfied Angela De Marco (Pfeiffer). Angela constantly bemoans her artificial lifestyle which revolves around her husband, 'Cucumber' Frank De Marco (Alec Baldwin), a middle-level mafioso who fills their home with tacky furniture and piles of electronic gadgetry, most of it still unwrapped, which, as Angela complains, not only fell off the back of a truck but also 'has blood on it'.

Frank's distaste for an honest life is apparent when he and a colleague travel on a commuter train, idly wondering how their fellow passengers can handle this kind of journey every working day. Frank's trip by train is a one-off; he's on board only because he has been ordered to kill one of the other passengers, like himself a minor villain.

Angela tells Frank that she wants a divorce but in this, as in everything else, he ignores her wishes. For one thing, mafia wives don't leave their husbands; for another, he has other fish to fry, being involved with Karen Lutnick (Nancy Travis). This dalliance is a very risky business because Karen is the mistress of Frank's boss, Tony 'the Tiger' Russo (Dean Stockwell), a man who is not prone to share what he believes to be his.

When Tony discovers what Frank is up to, he unhesitatingly kills him. The funeral brings together mobsters and their wives, including Tony's brassy, sharp-tongued, tough-minded, no-nonsense wife, Connie (Mercedes Ruehl). Later, Tony tries to step into Angela's life, buying her useless and unwanted gifts, like a costume for the dog, but she will have nothing to do with him and even moves out of her comfortable if tasteless home on Long Island to settle in a sleazy apartment on New York's Lower East Side. She takes with her only her young son, Joey (Anthony J. Nici), and a few clothes. To support herself and Joey, Angela takes a job as a hairdresser in a beauty parlour run by Rita Harcourt ('Sister' Carol East), who happens to be an illegal alien.

Tony orders his men to find Angela, partly because he still wants to get her into bed but also because he is aware that Angela might present a threat to him and his associates. As Frank De Marco's wife she must have learned many dangerous truths about the mob's activities; as his widow she no longer owes allegiance.

Meanwhile, all these moves have been followed with considerable interest by federal agents and two of them, Mike Downey and Ed Benitez (Matthew Modine and Oliver Platt) set up surveillance on Angela. Believing that they can exploit the situation to nail Tony, the agents bug Angela's apartment and Mike, in the guise of a food store employee, contrives to meet her and strike up a friendship.

Tony, who narrowly survives a hit by rival gangsters, eventually comes calling on Angela, unaware that his wife is watching him and suspects that the affair Tony desires is already in full swing. Instead, Connie sees Mike leaving Angela's apartment, grittily asking him, 'Whose husband are you, dogface?'.

Forced by the attentions of Tony and the threatening behaviour of Connie to spend the night with Mike, Angela tells him about herself and her life. Realizing now that Angela is not the kind of woman he had previously assumed her to be, Mike begins to revise his opinion of her and also to recognize the fact that he is falling in love. But Mike's boss, FBI Regional Director Franklin (Trey Wilson), is determined to send Tony Russo to prison and coerces Angela into helping them. If she doesn't, he threatens to have Rita deported.

Although Angela is angry with Mike's duplicity and uneasy with what the FBI want of her, she cannot risk hurting her new friends at the beauty parlour so she gives Tony a bugged ring and agrees to his latest request which is that she accompany him to Miami where he hopes to iron out the problems he is having with rival gang boss, Johnny 'Fisheggs' Roe (Ralph Corsel).

Connie, who is seeing Tony off at the airport, casually mentions that she has seen Angela with Mike. Although Tony has no intimation that Mike is a federal agent, he is made suddenly wary. After Tony departs, Connie learns that he has booked the honeymoon suite at his hotel in Miami and sets out in furious pursuit.

In Miami, events slip into high gear as Tony spots Mike. Although he recognizes him only as a face from Angela's apartment building, he takes Mike prisoner and then discovers the true purpose of the ring Angela gave him. Things look grim for Angela but she gets herself off the hook by revealing to Tony's comrades that it was he who murdered Frank. With his own people now turning against him, Tony's freedom is suddenly threatened by the arrival in force of the FBI. An even greater threat, this time to Tony's life, appears in the form of the irate Connie.

After a wild and woolly shoot-out, Tony is captured and is sent to prison while Angela returns to her job with Rita. Mike reappears in her life, hoping that she will forgive him for his original deception.

Throughout *Married to the Mob*, Jonathan Demme's sharp eye for detail is at work. The settings, be they the tackily expensive, mostly pink, furnishings of Angela's Long Island home or the tackily cheerful hairdressing establishment or the tackily cheap apartment building or the tackily gaudy honeymoon hotel suite, are wonderfully observed. But settings are worthless if the people occupying them are not right. Fortunately, they almost all are and Demme never makes the mistake of allowing even the smallest role to pass underdeveloped. Pretty nearly everyone looks right, dresses right, walks right, and talks right.

Pfeiffer commented upon the talking, praising her dialect

coach, Richard Ericson, but also recognizing the beneficial input she received from several real-life Long Island residents. A relative of Demme's, who lives on Long Island, asked some friends to record some of Pfeiffer's lines so that she could hear how the words sounded in their accents. And she befriended some Long Island hairdressers who not only helped polish her accent but also gave her valuable insights into their lives and behaviour. 'I met some great gals out in Long Island,' she remarked in interviews during which she adopted her Angela De Marco accent. 'They're fantastic. Cawla [Carla] and Anna Maria. They were sistuhs. Cawla was a hairdresser, she was going to be getting her own chair. We talked about hair, we talked about nails, we talked about make-up. I wanted to be more like them after I met them. Because they have a certain art of really enjoying life.'

Apart from the talk, she also spoke of the walk, explaining that Angela's way of walking was an exaggerated version of her own. 'My walk is constantly made fun of . . . by people who watch [me]. I should have been Howard the Duck.'

Although Pfeiffer could be highly self-critical of her abilities as a comic actress (to say nothing of her view of her looks), stating that she never thinks of herself as being funny, her performance in the film is not only funny it is also moving and strong and she is wholly in control as the mainstay. As *Variety* put it, she has 'never been better'.

Along with many talented young film-makers Jonathan Demme emerged from Roger Corman's hot-house school for unknown talent. For Corman he had written and directed some New World low-budget, tight-schedule schlock titles including *The Hot Box* (1972) and *Caged Heat* (1974). His innate humour and sense of character surfaced in *Citizens Band* (1977) and *Melvin and Howard* (1980) but fell foul of the power of producer-as-star with the Goldie Hawn feature, *Swing Shift* (1984). He returned to form, if not to box-office success, with *Something Wild* (1986) and *Miami Blues* (1990) and hit the commercial and critical jackpot in 1991 with *The Silence of the Lambs*.

Married to the Mob was seen by another Corman-graduate, director Martin Scorcese, who was so impressed at Pfeiffer's ability to get under the skin of the kind of people he grew up with that he mentally marked her down as someone to work with when the right opportunity arose; a fact which was to have highly significant repercussions a few years later.

Among Pfeiffer's supporting players, Baldwin does well as Angela's cheap-minded, ruthless, if short-lived husband. Production gossip linked him and Pfeiffer romantically but, then, that kind of rumour is very much par for the course in the motion-picture industry. Dean Stockwell is also excellent. This one-time child actor of distinction achieved the remarkable feat of coming back from the land where forgotten child actors go to become an exceptionally good player of character roles.

As the romantic lead opposite Pfeiffer, Modine was more than somewhat edged into the shade. Although his pale-faced, weak-willed character gave him little to develop, he rarely looked like the kind of man Angela would go for; unless, after life with Frank, she wanted the safety of dull routine. As Laurence Astor, writing in *Films and Filming*, remarked, 'Even the gorgeous Michelle Pfeiffer fails to move him overmuch; for affection Modine substitutes something like mild interest, a reaction likely to leave watching males in a state of severe perplexity.'

Of all the supporting players, the one most likely to leave watching males in a state of severe anxiety is Mercedes Ruehl as Connie Russo. Her strident, vengeful characterization provides the film with many of its high spots and she comes close to stealing every scene in which she appears. (Ruehl won an Oscar in 1991 for her role in *The Fisher King*.)

A poster in the window of the beauty parlour in *Married to the Mob* bears the slogan 'Are you ready for a brand new you?' and Pfeiffer certainly looks different. Sporting a mountainous wig that cascades dark brown curls around her face she was a world away from the cool blonde sophistication of real life. But in her next film role, she turned back to looking like herself and away from comedy.

In a sense, Pfeiffer's role in *Tequila Sunrise* (1988) was treading water. She simply does not have enough to do as the third side of a love interest triangle that competes a shade uneasily with another triangle of deceit and deception.

Written and directed by Robert Towne, *Tequila Sunrise* is set in Los Angeles with its plot rooted in drug smuggling and dealing. What it is really about, however, is the nature of friendship. Dale 'Mac' McKussick (Mel Gibson) is a reformed drugs dealer, trying to go straight and bring up his young son in a decent environment. Mac's wife left him when he made his decision to drop out of the drug business which was followed by a sharp decline in their standard of living.

Mac is persuaded to resume his activities for a one-off deal to help out a friend only to discover that it is a set-up engineered by another old friend, Nick Frescia (Kurt Russell), an agent with the federal narcotics agency. Nick does not believe that Mac is truly trying to go straight but, rather, that he is still up to his old tricks although managing to conceal things a little better than in the past. Another friend of Mac's is Lindroff (Arliss Howard), who is also trying to persuade him to resume trafficking. In fact, Lindroff has been planted by Nick's boss, Maguire (J. T. Walsh), who is determined to send Mac to prison.

While keeping Mac under surveillance, Nick discovers that he is spending a great deal of time with Jo Ann Vallenari (Pfeiffer), a restaurateur. At first, Nick convinces himself that Jo Ann is also involved in drugs. Eventually, he realizes that she is not only an entirely honest citizen, but that Mac is in love with her. In time, Nick is also attracted to Jo Ann and these three: Mac, Nick and Jo Ann form the first of the triangles.

The second triangle emerges when yet another old friend from Mac's past appears on the scene. A Mexican drugs agency officer, Escalante (Raul Julia), comes to Los Angeles to help Maguire and his men capture the mysterious Carlos, a leading Mexican trafficker. In fact, Escalante *is* Carlos and he and Mac know one another from a time they both were imprisoned in Mexico where Carlos saved Mac's life. This triangle, Mac, Carlos and Nick, is not only damaging to Mac's relationship with Jo Ann, it is also dangerously likely to put his life in jeopardy.

Carlos kills Lindroff and has similar plans for Jo Ann whom he believes can testify against himself and Mac. Instead, Mac imprisons Carlos on his boat, where he is also hiding several million dollars belonging to the Mexican. Planning to dispose of Carlos, Mac sabotages the boat's fuel system but then changes his mind. Carlos manages to escape, seizes a gun and tries to shoot Mac but is himself shot by Maguire, not quite the upright lawman he seems, who also tries to kill Mac. Nick arrives and kills Maguire in order to save his friend's life. During all the gunfire, the boat's damaged fuel system ignites and the boat explodes, with Mac apparently still on board.

The next morning, Mac reappears and meets Jo Ann. Nick watches in resignation as the couple are reunited, free from the dangers with which he helped surround them.

The complexities of the friendships and divided loyalties with which *Tequila Sunrise* abounds are seldom entirely clear. Despite the explosions of violent action, this is a very talkative film with each of the pairs of friends/lovers conversing endlessly about their feelings for one another and how these feelings are influenced by their other friendships.

Robert Towne's previous scriptwriting credits resulted in some excellent films, including *Chinatown* (1974), for which he won an Oscar, and *Shampoo* (1975), unsuccessfully Oscar-nominated. Perhaps director Towne was not as ruthless as he should have been with his own screenplay for *Tequila Sunrise*.

Despite all the talk, motives and real feelings remain muddied. Mac's reasons for going straight are uncertain and whatever he might have done in the past – which was presumably bad enough to cause all the interest being taken in him – is glossed over. Also hazy is the reason for Nick's friendship with Mac being so strong that he can risk his reputation, career and life for him.

Amidst all the often-inscrutable male-bonding, Pfeiffer appears cool and unruffled, except during a literally steamy love scene with Gibson which takes place in a circular hot tub that is remarkably visible to watching cops. *Variety* thought that she 'achieves a rather touching quality with her gun-shy girl beneath the polished professional'. However, her role is subservient to the other three members of the two triangles, but when she is on screen she certainly attracts attention although, like all the talk, much of the film has a dark and muddy look to it which often makes it quite difficult to discern who is doing what to whom. Even Jo Ann's restaurant, the obviously exclusive and expensive Vallenari, is so dimly lit that it's a wonder the customers can find the food on their plates.

Overall, Pfeiffer was not too pleased with the outcome, refusing to watch the finished film and occasionally indulging in mildly critical comments about the director, thus displaying feelings which are, it seems, mutual. Director Towne was ambivalent towards Pfeiffer. Setting up a dubious comparison to Grace Kelly, he said, 'You're constantly wondering what's underneath this almost Kelly-like cool.' On the whole, however, Towne was less than enamoured, asserting that Pfeiffer was the most difficult actress he'd ever worked with. For her part, Pfeiffer felt that he was the most difficult director she'd come under. She enjoyed working with Gibson who, she found, had a curious but compatible sense of humour. She also got on well with Russell, who she described as being one of the most married men she'd ever met, being completely wrapped up in his relationship with his wife, Goldie Hawn.

The ambience and setting of *Tequila Sunrise*, the world of drugs dealers and contemporary violence in Southern California, is aeons away from pre-Revolutionary France, which is where Pfeiffer's next role took her. It also took her to

Europe and into close contact with an actor with whom she developed an unusually close and, as it turned out, potentially damaging relationship. In the circumstances, the new film's title was uncomfortably close to real life.

Christopher Hampton based his screenplay for *Dangerous Liaisons* (1988) upon his own stage play, *Les Liaisons Dangereuses*, which he had adapted from the eighteenth-century novel by Chodleros de Laclos. The novel was published less than a decade before the French Revolution cleansed France, albeit with much blood, of the disagreeably vapid and morally bankrupt aristocracy de Laclos sought to unveil.

The story swirls like a poisonous whirlpool around the activities of the Marquise de Merteuil (Glenn Close) and the Viscomte de Valmont (John Malkovich), former lovers who now play dangerous games with the lives of others, using sex as their weapon.

The Marquise's latest lover is planning to leave her in order to marry the young and still virginal Cécile de Volanges (Uma Thurman). To revenge herself on this unacceptable slight, the Marquise asks Valmont to seduce Cécile before her wedding. But Valmont decides that this is too simple a task for a man with his reputation; he would be the laughing-stock of Paris were he to set his sights on such an easy target. Instead, the immoral pair devise a scheme whereby Valmont will seduce the prim and morally pure Madame de Tourvel (Pfeiffer) whose husband is away. Once the seduction is effected, Valmont's prize will be a resumption of his affair with the Marquise – something the Marquise's deserting lover will be informed of and which will make him the butt of derision.

Valmont visits Madame de Tourvel who is staying at the country house of his aunt, Madame de Rosemonde (Mildred Natwick), and begins persuading her that he is now a reformed character and anxious to live down his reputation as a philanderer. He makes only slow progress but then matters are prodded by the actions of the Marquise. Still eager to have Cécile deflowered before her wedding, the Marquise introduces the young woman to Chevalier Dancény (Keanu Reeves), a music teacher. Although Dancény promptly falls in love with Cécile, he nobly refuses to persuade her to relinquish her virginity to him.

Meanwhile, Valmont's lack of progress with Madame de Tourvel is hindered still further when Cécile's mother, Madame de Volanges (Swoosie Kurtz), writes warning letters to his prey. The Marquise now arranges for Cécile to be sent to the house in the country where she guesses, rightly, that Valmont will seduce her after all. Valmont finds Cécile an eager and willing participant in her own seduction but by now Madame de Tourvel has fallen in love with him. From somewhere, however, Valmont finds a tiny spark of decency and turns away from her submissiveness.

Back in Paris, the Marquise taunts Valmont for what she regards as a weakness; in her depraved world allowing the heart to overrule the mind is contemptible. Yet, for all her acid comments, the Marquise is regretting the fact that she and Valmont are no longer lovers and have to play these games with one another before she can justify a resumption in their relationship.

Valmont's response to the Marquise's taunting is to return to Madame de Tourvel and carry out his original plan. After seducing her, he goes to the Marquise who now insists on written evidence, a letter from Madame de Tourvel which declares her love for him. The Marquise also condemns Valmont for the fact that he is clearly in love with the other woman. Valmont obtains such a letter from Madame de Tourvel and breaks off their relationship and as a result she falls ill with despair and is cared for by nuns who bleed her in the hope of a cure.

Back in Paris, the Marquise has taken Dancény as her latest lover and when Cécile has a miscarriage she tells the young man the part Valmont has played in all this. Dancény challenges Valmont to a duel and wounds the older man who turns away the attentions of a doctor and dies. Dancény hurries to Madame de Tourvel's bedside where she is now nearing death. Dancény assures her that Valmont really loved her but she closes her eyes and dies.

The Marquise boldly visits the Paris Opéra but the audience, aware now of how far she has gone in her damaging and dangerous liaisons, turns wrathfully upon her.

In some respects the moralistic undertones of *Dangerous Liaisons* reflect events in contemporary society (European if not necessarily American) although, as Tom Milne observed, writing in *Monthly Film Bulletin*, this is a 'far cry from the sharp scalpel Chodleros de Laclos wielded to demonstrate the layers of callus grown over the affluent heart which made the French Revolution . . . a foregone conclusion'.

The changes made by Hampton to de Laclos's work, in part necessitated by adaptation to other media, removes much of the original's political message. Although de Laclos was himself a member of the aristocracy, he was sufficiently far-sighted to acknowledge the inevitability of the fall from power of his class which by behaviour such as that depicted in his novel showed that it had not only fallen from grace but had also proved itself to be a worthless burden upon the state. It might be that much the same could be said of certain aspects of European society in the 1980s, particularly that of Britain. But politics are not something with which the film concerns itself.

Dangerous Liaisons works extremely well in its depiction of individuals, bereft of emotion, idle beyond belief, driven to while away their lives by damaging others, seeking titillation not only from their own sexual dalliances but also from voyeuristically driving others to perform acts which run against whatever moral standards they might possess.

Stephen Frears' direction is controlled and sensitive. After many years directing for BBC television, Frears had moved into independent productions (sometimes in association with BBC2 or Channel 4) which were often small-scale and beautifully observed studies of sexuality. Amongst his successes are *Gumshoe* (1972), *My Beautiful Launderette* (1985),

Sammy and Rosie Get Laid and the story of Joe Orton, *Prick Up Your Ears* (both 1987).

Visually, *Dangerous Liaisons* is very pleasing to the eye and shows few signs of having been opened up from a stage play. Hampton's script is elegant and eloquent but never wordy. His characters have lines which depend heavily upon the actors' skills with cadence and weight as much as any nuances resulting from closely observed facial expressions or body language.

Pfeiffer commented upon the problems of language she encountered on the film, doubtless highlighted by having come to it after quite recently working on a very different kind of language problem in her role as Angela De Marco. Reported by William Green in London's *Sunday Telegraph*, she said, 'I don't have a Shakespearean background, so I had to learn a whole new language of rhythm and stylized delivery.'

She enters wholly into the character of the doomed young woman she portrays, suffering with such intensity that when she is bled by nuns as she lies on her deathbed she seems to dwindle and fade before the eyes. Her own eyes, which she often asserts are naturally a trace bloodshot, are swollen with tears as her emotional agony takes the life from her.

Director Stephen Frears was very impressed with Pfeiffer, remarking on her 'wonderfully expressive face' and thinking that working with her gave him some hint of what it might have been like in the past working with Greta Garbo, adding, 'She seems born to be in the movies.'

Variety liked her, too, declaring that 'Pfeiffer makes a fragile, touching Madame de Tourvel, as her suffering under Valmont's incessant pressure becomes palpable.' Pauline Kael, doyenne of American film critics, described Pfeiffer as paradisially beautiful, going on to say that 'when she breaks down crying, she's helplessly human, a real person caught in a maze of deception.'

Praise showered in from all quarters and amongst the many results was her nomination for an Academy Award as

Best Supporting Actress. (The Oscar went to Geena Davis for *The Accidental Tourist*.)

Amongst the other supporting players, Uma Thurman enters engagingly into the spirit of the sensual innocent, Cécile, while Swoosie Kurtz and that splendid old trouper Mildred Natwick fill their roles with charm and skill.

Glenn Close and John Malkovich, the two principals, carry the film's weight and perform superbly. Malkovich brings to his role a brooding intensity that clearly reflects the passion of a man willing and able to use his sexuality in the manner of Valmont's choice. Bewigged and powdered in the fashion of the times he may be, but he exudes male sexual dominance. Early in his career, Malkovich was a member of the Chicago-based Steppenwolf Theatre Company and he also worked in New York, directing and acting in both contemporary and classical drama on and off-Broadway before entering films.

At the time of making *Dangerous Liaisons*, Malkovich had been married for some years to actress Glenne Headley but was reputed to have a powerful effect upon women. He had such an effect on Pfeiffer and they entered into a short-lived but intense relationship. He left his wife and Pfeiffer ended her affair with Michael Keaton. But Malkovich eventually returned to his wife and Pfeiffer, emotionally bruised and drained from both the film and the affair, returned to America and subsequently avoided any public appearance connected with the film that might have led to her being brought face-to-face with him. She even chose not to attend a London screening of the film attended by the Princess of Wales.

For all the outstanding displays of acting from Pfeiffer and Malkovich, heightened as they were by their personal involvement, the film's most dominant figure is undoubtedly Glenn Close. Her glacial, heartless, endlessly scheming bitch is a brilliant display of calculated menace. With her hair pulled tightly back from her face, this emphasizing her predatory expression, her breasts pushed up into revealing cleavage in the corseted manner of the period, Close looks the very image of a threatening, dangerous, sexual weapon. Interestingly, she is just as threatening in her deliberate coldness as she was as the white-hot 'other woman' in the 1987 film *Fatal Attraction*.

Close's performance, made all the more remarkable because only seven weeks before shooting started she had given birth to her daughter, earned her a nomination for an Academy Award as Best Actress.

Pfeiffer's nomination for an Oscar, although unsuccessful, came somewhat unsurprisingly; *Dangerous Liaisons* does, after all, bear all the hallmarks of a 'quality' film. That she should be nominated again for an Oscar the following year was itself unusual; given the type of film it was, on the surface, this was even more surprising.

The Fabulous Baker Boys (1989) is at once hard to categorize and somehow comfortably familiar to anyone who has been watching films since before the 1970s when slam-bam-thank-you-ma'am sex and action movies took over as box-office front-runners.

Not that there is a dated look or feel to the film which tells a simple, slightly predictable story, makes no pretensions to be anything more than entertainment, but does all this with flair and polish. Everything about it is never less than good, mostly very good indeed, and some of the time it is truly excellent.

Frank and Jack Baker (Beau and Jeff Bridges) are pianists on the cabaret circuit. Based in Seattle, they gently tinkle out their stale repertoire of show tunes to audiences who are not there to listen but to eat or drink or talk, usually loudly enough to drown out the music. For Frank, devoted to his family, the work is what he needs to keep his home life stable and his financial head above the waters. For Jack, a solitary individual with an eye for the ladies, just so long as they are never more than one-night stands, the work is crushingly boring. The way in which they play the songs is Frank's idea; melodically, unimaginatively and dull. Jack, at heart a jazz-man, wants to stamp the music with his own personality.

For all the differences between the brothers, both are agreed on one thing – bookings are falling and unless they do something soon they will be out of business. Frank, the duo's businessman, has an idea; they will add a girl singer to the act. Jack couldn't care less.

Auditioning singers turns out to be a depressing disaster as, one after another, girls and young women troop into a gloomy rehearsal room and prove just how bad some singers can be. With thirty-seven no-hopers seen and heard and dismissed, Frank and Jack start wearily to pack up but then a late arrival stumbles through the door. Unsteady on a broken heel, clad in voluminous, scruffy clothes and with hair that looks as if it has been freshly knitted for the occasion, this is Susie Diamond (Pfeiffer). She is only allowed to sing after she harangues the brothers into submission and, to their astonishment, however unpolished she might be, Susie really is good.

Despite her promise, Jack is wary. Much as he dislikes the act the way it is now, he doesn't like the thought of adding a girl. Maybe he isn't too happy at the thought of becoming successful and having to keep on playing the cabaret circuit. Most of all, he is suspicious that Susie's previous job, working for the Triple-A Escort Service, merely thinly disguises the fact that she's a hooker.

The brothers push Susie through hasty rehearsals and an even hastier course in grooming. On her opening night, fearful that she will forget the songs, Susie wears a 'bracelet' of cue cards, sneaks a quick drink from a passing waiter, and takes her place at the microphone only to find that it is incorrectly adjusted. As she wrestles with it, Frank hisses instructions and she snaps, 'What fucking switch?', which is heard by everyone in the room thus startling her first audience into paying attention.

As the brothers begin to play the opening bars of 'Ten Cents a Dance' disaster strikes when Susie's bracelet breaks and all her cue cards are scattered on the floor. As she scrabbles around for them, the moment comes for her entry.

Panic-stricken, Frank opens his mouth to sing but then, miraculously, Susie's voice is heard as she rises gracefully, right on cue, and becomes an instant hit with the usually blasé audience.

The act's reputation is restored and bookings soar but dissension begins creeping in. Both the brothers like Susie. Frank, the older brother, sees her much as he sees Jack, as a younger relative he must protect. For years Frank, aware of Jack's attitude towards women, has sometimes come close to pimping for his brother. But this is different and he doesn't want Jack to treat Susie as if she's just another one-night stand. Jack's home life, such as it is, revolves around his elderly Labrador and a little girl from an adjoining apartment whose mother leaves her home all day while she works. Now, he finds in Susie someone with whom he can share more than just sex but he is still worried about her work as an 'escort'. Was it just a fancy name for a call-girl? And is she still doing it? When Frank warns Jack to stay away from Susie a rift begins to form between the brothers.

A New Year booking finds Jack and Susie working alone; Frank has decided to spend time with his family. Susie, clad in a revealing red dress, slinks and slides provocatively across the top of Jack's grand piano for a performance of 'Makin' Whoopee' that puts new life and meaning into the old song. Almost inevitably, after such an arousing perform-ance, Jack and Susie end the evening making love.

Despite their success, the brothers are still at odds over the repertoire. 'Makin' Whoopee', Susie-style, is not what Frank wants and soon not only is Jack bored with it but so is Susie. When she is offered a job singing commercials in television, she seriously considers leaving the act. Although he knows what it will mean to them if she goes, Frank reluctantly advises her to take the job. Annoyed that he didn't try persuading her to stay, Susie quits and the brothers become a piano duo again.

An invitation to appear on a charity telethon is accepted by Frank but it turns out to be a cheapskate operation run by a neighbourhood television station. Treated like the rest of the, mostly untalented artists on the show, Jack finally erupts and walks out. In an alley, Frank and Jack argue and then fight but eventually come to an understanding. Soon, when Jack announces that he is quitting the act to play piano in a jazz club, Frank offers no resistance.

Jack and Susie meet up again: 'Hey, am I gonna see you again?' – 'What do you think?' – 'Yeah, I think I am gonna see you again.'

The film marks the directorial debut of Steve Kloves and it is a wonderful first outing. From the outset, Kloves establishes a pace that while leisurely never becomes slow and his camera placing is flawless. The moment when Susie rises up into shot as she launches into 'Ten Cents a Dance' is a case in point. Also well-conceived and effectively accomplished is a long sequence in which the trio occupy adjoining hotel rooms and the camera weaves in and out as Frank nostalgically recalls his early days in the business before he and then Jack dance with Susie.

The music, also perfectly appropriate, is under the guidance of Dave Grusin, himself a jazz pianist turned record producer and impresario (and in 1993 back on the jazz circuit again). Grusin also dubbed the piano track for Jeff Bridges while John F. Hammond dubbed for Beau Bridges, the actors being coached by pianists Joyce Collins and Lou Foresteri.

The idea of a jazzman forced to play cocktail lounge piano might appear to be another Hollywood cliché but the great jazz pianist Johnny Guarnieri was obliged to do just that. From the late 1970s until his death in 1985 he played at the Hollywood Plaza Hotel and on the piano-bar at The Tail of the Cock, a restaurant on Ventura Boulevard. Obliged by the requirements of the job, Guarnieri carefully kept his enormous talent under wraps so as not to offend customers who were there to be heard, not to listen.

Coached by Sally Stevens, Michelle Pfeiffer did her own singing and makes a remarkably good job of it. During the build-up to the shooting of the film, she worked hard on this aspect of her performance. Although she had sung in *Grease 2*, this kind of singing was a very different matter. As a solo singer backed only by two discreet pianos, there is no place to hide and she had to be good. 'For this picture,' she said, 'I listened to a lot of music – Billie Holiday, Helen Merrill. I didn't copy anybody, but I heard a lot.' Certainly, there is no sign of an attempt to sound like Holiday (which would have been disastrous) or Merrill (an exceptionally good and very under-rated singer), but Pfeiffer somehow finds the right touch for a girl like Susie Diamond; not quite a jazz singer but much more attuned to the nuances of a songwriter's intentions than show and pop singers who, as a general rule, sell themselves not the song. Susie is clearly superior to the milieu in which she works, but not so good that she isn't already in the big time. It is a remarkably accurate, perceptive and convincing performance.

Despite the hard work involved in creating the right character for Susie and preparing the vocal side of her role, Pfeiffer learned to relax through working with Jeff Bridges, declaring that he 'taught me how to have fun acting. Before I could never let my guard down. I was very serious, concentrated, focused, Jeff would say, "Hell, do you want to play cards?"'

She was also casually dismissive of her performance, especially of the much-talked-about 'Makin' Whoopee' scene: 'It's hard to take yourself seriously, when you're slinking around on a piano.' Nevertheless, director Kloves said that she is 'someone who constantly wants to improve herself and widen her appreciation of the world. You shouldn't underestimate this girl.'

Reviewers were not underestimating her. David Ansen, in *Newsweek*, commented, 'Pfeiffer has never been more alluring. She is slinky, brittle perfection.'

Variety summed up her performance succinctly: 'She's dynamite.'

She certainly was, and the critics responded with a string of awards including Best Actress from the Golden Globes, the American National Board of Review, and the Film Critics' associations of Los Angeles and New York, and the National Society of Film Critics.

Amongst the actresses who didn't get the role of Susie Diamond was Madonna, who was later highly critical of the film. Pfeiffer shrugged off these well-publicized remarks: 'I think Madonna is peeved that it has been such a huge success. I can only put it down to sour grapes.'

Singing is, of course, only part of what Pfeiffer does in the film. The off-stage side of Susie is an intriguing and often conflicting mixture of strident vulgarity and subdued vulnerability. Pfeiffer handles these shifts with subtlety and conviction.

As the younger, wayward Baker boy, Jeff Bridges gives a quietly eloquent performance, underlining the fact that he is one of the best actors in Hollywood who is only rarely given parts worthy of his ability. Perhaps his on-screen diffidence marks him down in some eyes. His older brother, Beau, was a former child actor, appearing in several films before quitting for a while to attempt a sporting career. Back in films from the early 1960s, his round-faced youthfulness restricted the kind of parts he was offered but as he matured he began to achieve success as a character actor of distinction. Both brothers (their father is veteran actor Lloyd Bridges, their mother actress Dorothy Simpson) submerge themselves completely in their roles and are thoroughly believable as the piano-playing partners.

Inevitably, however, it was Pfeiffer who attracted most attention but, despite the numerous awards she did win, her Academy Award nomination as Best Actress was unsuccessful, the Oscar going to Jessica Tandy for *Driving Miss Daisy*.

Although the past year had been fraught with difficult personal problems, Pfeiffer had more than compensated with her film work. By any standards, her performances in *Married to the Mob*, *Dangerous Liaisons* and *The Fabulous Baker Boys* were exceptional. That they should have come in such quick succession and were so highly individualistic removed any lingering doubts there might have been that she was not only here to stay but was a superstar and a box-office certainty all wrapped inside a hugely talented actress. Only a short while before, Carson Black had observed in the London *Times*, that she was a 'star with Hollywood at her feet [but] is still waiting to be taken seriously'. Now Hollywood was taking her very seriously indeed. All doors were open; she could do anything she wanted. She had achieved something countless actresses before had striven after. As she said, 'When I first went into the business, someone told me that being able to turn a part down was the only thing that would ever give me power.'

Now, she had power.

6 *From Katya to Catwoman*

Michelle Pfeiffer's background as an actress does not include the stage. True, her learning period included some minor moments on the boards, in small productions, but nothing of consequence. On the surface, therefore, her acceptance of an invitation to play Olivia in *Twelfth Night* during a Shakespeare festival in New York City seems an odd decision.

Although there are a number of Shakespeare festivals in various states (and a notable tradition in Canada), the Bard's works fall outside the mainstream of American theatre. Nevertheless, as in any English-speaking country (and some others, especially Russia), to play in Shakespeare adds an important entry to an actor's track record, bringing with it a certain cachet to say nothing of instilling important disciplines and understanding of language and drama.

Perhaps Pfeiffer's decision was rooted in a personal characteristic which she has commented upon in interviews; the need to take on roles which frighten her.

Not that the run up to *Twelfth Night* suggested that this would be a frightening project. Rehearsals for Joseph Papp's production went well and she was comforted by the presence of other film actors including two she had worked with in the past: Jeff Goldblum, her co-star from *Into the Night*, and Mary Elizabeth Mastrantonio, one of her few female allies on *Scarface*.

However, the play was to be staged in Central Park's Delacorte Theatre and on opening night she found herself gazing over footlights not at a handful of friends but an eager, star-struck audience of almost 2,000. Pfeiffer later commented that she had looked 'forward to it as a personal

growth experience [but] I'd never anticipated such attention'. Nevertheless, she found it an enriching experience. It
was 'exciting and fun and exploding and horrifying, with
some fighting'.

The critics were largely unkind, some having formed advance opinions based largely upon the widely held assump-
tion that movie stars are unsuited for the legitimate theatre.
This, and the theory that Papp was more interested in publicity than an accurate rendering of the play, gave them lots
of ammunition. In the event, despite some pithily derogatory
reviews, the play ran its scheduled four weeks and attracted
good audiences (it was, after all, free).

Amongst the cast was a young stage actor named Fisher
Stevens, quite well known within the narrow confines of the
off-Broadway fringe. Although several years her junior, he
and Pfeiffer hit it off well and despite her determination to
stay on the west coast and work in films and his to stay in the
east, and on the stage, they formed a close relationship which
rumours held might lead to marriage.

Stevens even visited her on location for her next role, as a
Russian editor in the film version of a John Le Carré novel.

The film of *The Russia House* (1990) is caught in the hiatus
between the Cold War and whatever might happen post-
glasnost/perestroika, and some of the political weight
charted in the novel disappears. Instead of treating Le
Carré's events as a historical narrative (admittedly very difficult because this particular piece of the past is so close and
its determination still uncertain), the screenplay, by Tom
Stoppard, simply accommodates recent events with a few
'business as usual' lines from the assembled British and
American espionage agents.

Katya Orlova (Pfeiffer), an editor with a Russian publishing house, visits a Moscow book fair, hoping to meet a British
publisher named Barley Blair but his stand is deserted. He
hasn't bothered to come. Reluctantly, Katya asks the man on
an adjoining stand, Niki Landau (Nicholas Woodeson), to
take a manuscript back to London with him and hand it over

to Blair. Landau agrees but after reading the manuscript takes it instead to British Intelligence.

The work, which is of unknown authorship, is an apparently genuine account of the Russian nuclear capability with all its weaknesses carefully delineated. British and American intelligence forces decide to work together on the matter, led respectively by Ned (James Fox) and Russell (Roy Scheider).

Their first decision is to talk to Barley Blair (Sean Connery) who prefers to live in the sun in Lisbon rather than beaver away at his publishing business in London. Eventually, Ned and Russell decide that Blair is being truthful when he tells them that he has no idea who the author of the manuscript might be or why he was chosen as its recipient. He does, however, hazard a guess that it might be a man he met some years before and who goes by the name of 'Dante'.

Unimpressed by and mildly contemptuous of the agents, Blair agrees to go to Russia, contact Katya, and try, through her, to meet the author and confirm the manuscript's authenticity and accuracy.

Blair is immediately attracted to Katya and although at first cautious of him she gradually responds. She arranges a meeting with Dante (Klaus Maria Brandauer), in reality a man named Savelev, her former lover who is now a leading atomic scientist. Given a list of questions to ask Dante which will help the Western agents determine his veracity and potential usefulness, Blair proceeds with his mission all the while falling more in love with Katya.

Then, by way of a coded telephone call, Katya learns that Dante, who has been very ill for some time, is dead. Perhaps it was natural causes, perhaps not. Neither Katya nor Blair can tell because, as Blair is rapidly realizing, he has become involved in a duplicitous business in which no one can be trusted. Now, Blair learns that the Russians are not only already aware of Dante's manuscript but are also playing cold war games. What is more, neither the Russians nor the British-American alliance care what happens to Katya.

During an embassy party, after Blair has indulged his

passion for jazz by playing soprano saxophone with the band, he speaks to a Russian friend who has many official contacts. Through him, he arranges to hand over the list of questions he is supposed to ask Dante, thus providing the Russians with clues to gaps in the West's knowledge of the balance of nuclear capability.

Watched by agents of all sides, Blair goes through the motions of meeting Dante while Ned is growingly suspicious of him. Russell, however, insists that they stay with their original plan, barely able to believe that someone who is not a member of the intelligence services, least of all a saxophone-playing publisher, could outfox them.

Blair enters the building where he has told Ned and Russell that Dante is waiting, hands over the list to a Russian agent, and is allowed to quietly disappear. No longer of any use to either side, Blair returns to Lisbon to await 'payment' from the Russians for his betrayal of his own side. Some weeks later his payment is made when he is joined by Katya and her family.

Steadfastly low-key, *The Russia House* frequently promises much more than it delivers. The sniping between the British and American intelligence and government officials is amusing and often pointed. There is a high-camp performance by Ken Russell and one of oily menace by Michael Kitchen, but all are too obviously set up to be the bad guys. In contrast, the Russians, either cuddly or delightfully earthy and totally trustworthy, are equally obviously the goodies. Perhaps this view (which to some extent reflects Le Carré's work) compensates for the years of 'red menace' movies when everything and everyone behind the iron curtain was deemed to be evil; but reality is surely that both sides have good and bad amongst the general population while both sides' intelligence services have clearly much to answer for before either can be taken on trust.

Supporting performances are mainly good, especially by Fox and Kitchen, although Scheider's foul-mouthed CIA agent goes a little over the top as he makes him as unpleasant as he can.

As Katya, Pfeiffer looks the very personification of a well-educated Muscovite and her accent, and some Russian dialogue she speaks, are wholly convincing (at least to non-Russian ears). She was aided in her work on her accent by an interpreter and remarked that she had partly based her character on this same young woman. Even so, she found the task very demanding: 'I've done dialects before, but this particular accent was very hard for me to retain.' *Variety* was impressed with the results, commenting that her 'accent proves very believable, and one is drawn to the lovely actress . . .'.

Overall, Pfeiffer found working on the film difficult. Although staying at the Sovietskaya Hotel, she soon learned that recent changes in Russian society – this was, of course, when Mikhail Gorbechev was still in power at the Kremlin – had not penetrated down to the ordinary men and women at street level. At one point during filming she discovered that the Russian authorities were applying a rule which forbade visiting film companies from providing food for Russian extras. Angered by this, she stormed off the set, later declaring herself disgusted with regulations which forced poorly paid extras, who were surrounded by shops with little or no food in them, to watch as visitors ate and drank to their hearts' content. What better proof could there be of the iniquities and inequalities of the suddenly in-favour capitalist state. Eventually, Pfeiffer backed down after officials persuaded her that this was the way things were and there was nothing she, nor anyone else for that matter, could do about it.

She turned this moral setback to her advantage, using in her role as Katya the realization that 'a Soviet woman is still much more passive than an American woman. It's still a very patriarchal culture.'

Forces external to the film crew were not the only pressures. She found director Fred Schepisi's decision to shoot some scenes in public places without pre-arrangement somewhat disconcerting. He would simply 'shove us in amongst the people and roll the camera. That was difficult.'

For all the on-location problems, however, Pfeiffer turns in a very good and generally believable performance. The only area where suspension of disbelief becomes troublesome is the love affair between Katya and Blair. It is easy to see why this ageing Britisher would fall for her, almost at first sight; it is much less clear why she should fall for him before getting to know what lurks beneath his boozy, bulky and bombastic exterior.

As has been pointed out elsewhere, an age difference can be a problem, although not inevitably so since men and women with an almost thirty-year age gap can find a true and close bond. But it is a difference that would surely give a girl pause for thought.

Some reports hinted that Pfeiffer and Connery 'failed to get on' but during pre-release press conferences there were no signs of any lingering antipathy. Indeed, Pfeiffer contradicted such reports when she commented that the first time she met Connery she was 'thoroughly intimidated – he's so *big*! He's an enormous man. And he has an incredibly powerful presence that just takes control of the whole room. But he defused the situation pretty quickly, and quite disarmed me, in fact. We got along very well.'

For his part, Connery makes the most of a roundly developed role. He might not look like a candidate for spy material – which Blair clearly isn't – but he certainly looks the part of a self-confident, bleary-eyed, brusque, authority-hating bombast. It is an enjoyable role for an actor and he makes the most of it. He even makes a credible job of pretending to play the soprano saxophone (which was dubbed for him by the brilliant young jazz star, Branford Marsalis, whose playing in the Connery sequences gives an appreciative nod to old master Sidney Bechet, while in the title sequences he is his distinctive contemporary self).

During the making of *The Russia House*, Sean Connery was voted the Sexiest Man Alive in one of those mindless polls that degrade just about everyone. Connery was then aged sixty. As Pfeiffer, then thirty-two, ruefully observed, she could never imagine the day when she, at sixty, would be allowed to have an on-screen love affair with a man half her age let alone be voted the sexiest woman alive.

Australian director Schepisi draws good performances from his actors, allowing them considerable latitude. The fact that he has twice directed Meryl Streep in excellent perform-ances suggests that he may be one of the, currently rare, male directors who are worthy successors to Frank Borzage, George Cukor, Victor Fleming, Douglas Sirk and other women's film specialists of the past.

Back in Hollywood from her excursion behind the fallen curtain, Pfeiffer was inundated with offers of important and generally very good roles. In one instance, that sign of strength – the ability to turn down a role – was centred upon a film which, in fact, contained one of the best roles for a woman to come along in years.

Jonathan Demme, with whom she had made *Married to the Mob*, wanted her for the role of FBI agent Clarice Starling in a film he was preparing from Thomas Harris's novel, *The Silence of the Lambs*. Pfeiffer passed, citing as her reason, that she was 'nervous of the subject matter. I was concerned about the glorification of serial killers – not that they glorified it, but I did think that Anthony Hopkins' part was the most charming and smartest.' Pfeiffer's partner, Kate Guinzburg, wanted her to take the role, no doubt sensing that the film was a potential smash-hit, but Pfeiffer remained adamant.

After *The Silence of the Lambs* had won Oscars for Hopkins as Best Actor and Jodie Foster as Best Actress, in the role Pfeiffer had turned down, this film was one of several named in a renewed censorship campaign.

Some time later, Pfeiffer met Anthony Hopkins and re-marked that in one way, at least, she was sorry not to have taken the part of Clarice Starling. 'I thought, darn, I'd have loved to have worked with you.'

The film Pfeiffer chose to make instead of *The Silence of the*

Lambs was *Love Field*, a project especially dear to her heart
and with which she had been involved for some time. Financial problems hit the studio backing the film and its release
was delayed for almost two years. This film will be discussed
in a later chapter.

With work on *Love Field* completed, Pfeiffer then went into
Garry Marshall's *Frankie and Johnny* (1991). Terrence
McNally based his screenplay for the film on his own stage
play, *Frankie and Johnny in the Clair de Lune*, which opened at
the off-Broadway Manhattan Theatre Club on 2 June 1987 for
an eighteen-month run. In the play, the protagonists (actually the sole performers as it was a two-hander) were middle-aged, plain, and very ordinary people, played by Kathy
Bates and F. Murray Abraham. Where the play was set in
Frankie's shabby, one-room New York apartment, the film
opens out to include many scenes in the Apollo, a steamy
fast-food joint, and out on the city's streets. There are also
scenes of Johnny leaving prison and Frankie visiting her
family. The cast list, too, was broadened; an additional
ninety-four people appearing in the screen version.

Frankie and Johnny (Pfeiffer and Al Pacino) are two lonely
people. He is just out of prison and looking for a job as a
short-order cook; she is still damaged from an unhappy and
violent relationship and is a waitress at the Apollo where he
comes to work.

Johnny is immediately struck by her, seeing that beneath
the wan, weary and unhappy surface lies a woman who
could, with just a little effort, be fairly attractive. Frankie, still
scarred from her last relationship, isn't looking for anyone
and barely notices him.

Johnny quickly becomes popular with the Apollo's owner,
Nick (Hector Elizondo), and the other waitresses: Nedda
(Jane Morris), the aggressively sexual Cora (Kate Nelligan),
and the older, out-on-her-feet Helen (Goldie McLaughlin).
But despite charming everyone in sight, Johnny fails to move
Frankie. When Helen collapses and dies, the other waitresses
are pleasantly surprised that Johnny, the new arrival, takes

the trouble to come to her funeral. Later, Johnny and Cora have a one-night stand but he still wants Frankie and sets out on a campaign to draw her out of her self-imposed isolation.

Eventually, encouraged by her close friends, Tim and Bobby (Nathan Lane and Sean O'Bryan), who share a neighbouring apartment, Frankie lets Johnny take her on a night out with the Apollo's staff. But being together at work or in a bowling alley is no way to let the pair draw closer and eventually Johnny's insistence wearies Frankie and she pushes him away, telling him:

'You don't know me.

'Of course I don't know you. You don't know me either. We got off to a great start. Why do you want to stop? What do you want? What do you want from a guy?'

'I want a guy who'll love me no matter what.'

'You got him.'

'Shit. This is worse than *Looking for Mr Goodbar*.'

Johnny, too, is isolated but in his case not from choice. His whole life until now has been a mess. His sense of isolation is made worse when he buys gifts for his children but on arriving at the house sees his ex-wife happy with her new husband and the kids happy too. He watches them for a while but he cannot bear even to climb from his car to speak to them.

Johnny insistently resumes his courtship of Frankie:

'Something's going on between us, something important. Don't you feel it?'

'I don't know what I feel.'

'You don't want to feel it. We're talking about two people coming together; sure it's a little scary, but it's fucking wonderful, too.'

But for all his determination, Frankie maintains her defences, even when he tells her:

'I want to go upstairs. Watch you get ready for bed, then climb in and make love to you for ten hours.'

'You expect me to be fooled with a line like that?'

But, finally, Frankie decides that she might risk setting

aside her fears that if she allows Johnny into her life he will hurt her. The film ends on a note of restrained optimism; maybe things will work out for them, maybe they won't, but at least they'll take another shot at finding happiness.

In many ways, *Frankie and Johnny* is an old-fashioned love story in the tradition of the big studios and in the past might have teamed any one of a dozen star players. It would not have looked the same, of course; not in the 1930s or '40s. Joan Crawford might have dressed down for a while, or even Lana Turner, but long before the final credits she would have donned full war-paint (as, for example, Crawford did in *Mildred Pierce*). And while James Stewart or even Robert Taylor might have played a short-order cook, neither would have looked down-at-heel, grubby and sweat-stained.

The decision to cast Pfeiffer and Pacino, and their determination to look ordinary, cannot fully hide the fact that they are people with strong characters and have the vitality that makes them stars. Disguise it though they do, and generally make a very good job of it, their star quality never fully vanishes beneath the steam and grease of their work in the diner.

Although some critics felt it harmed the concept, this residue of attractiveness is not detrimental. As Pfeiffer commented, the original stage script 'described Frankie as someone who could be attractive if she just put a little effort into how she looks. I don't look that good if I don't wear make-up.'

It is easy to understand why Pfeiffer, who usually takes a long time to reach a decision over a part, jumped at this one. She had taken the screenplay on to a flight she was making to Canada, to see Fisher Stevens, and when she arrived immediately called Garry Marshall to say she wanted the role. The story, old-fashioned though it might be in a Hollywood sense, has considerable depth. It is about human nature and how even those who have been badly misused somehow find the courage to make another attempt, however risky, at starting over. As Pfeiffer remarked, 'Frankie is somebody who's terribly wounded and believes that for her, in this lifetime, it's just not going to happen. And that intrigued me.'

The two leads play well together, with no scene-stealing and a comfortable sense of the reality of their initially stiff but slowly thawing relationship. They even found it possible to overcome the fact that Pfeiffer usually hits her stride by the third take while Pacino prefers seven or eight times that number.

The two stars enjoyed their reunion; in the eight years since *Scarface*, Pfeiffer had matured and Pacino had mellowed. Interviewed shortly before the film was released, Pfeiffer remarked on how she had been terrified on their first film together. Then, Pacino had been brooding and withdrawn and appeared to barely notice the woman who played his wife. This time it was different. 'I told Al,' Pfeiffer said, 'that he had become much nicer, and I had become much meaner. He's much more relaxed these days. And I've become a real bitch.' Pacino acknowledged that he might not have been very forthcoming at their first meeting: 'Maybe I was just a jerk, and I didn't know it.'

For all the new-found compatibility, there were problems. In scene 105 Frankie agrees to bare her breasts for Johnny. Pfeiffer hated doing the scene, declaring, 'It was very difficult for me. I was really a pain in the ass when we shot it.' The crew worked on the scene for three days before they had it right. By then, Pfeiffer said, she 'had become, well, *very* cranky'. Pacino was also wearied by the scene: 'I was so tired, sometimes my head would start drooping and it would get into the shot'.

After the scene was finally in the can, some of the technicians, all of them by now word perfect, made a gag reel with a dozen or more taking Pfeiffer's role and director Garry Marshall handed out specially printed T-shirts bearing the slogan: I SURVIVED SCENE 105.

Such difficulties as those experienced filming that particular scene do not show in the finished product. Pfeiffer's performance is well-balanced throughout and she creates just the right manner for a young woman who thinks she has settled for a solitary life only to discover, and at first fight against this discovery, that she really does need the caring and companionship the right man might bring her.

Considering that apart from the two leads every other character in the film is new to the story, they are all remarkably well-developed even if some are more than a trifle clichéd. Particularly good are Elizondo as the gruff but warm-hearted restaurant owner; Lane as Frankie's warm-hearted homosexual neighbour, the only man with whom, right now, she can feel at ease; and all the Apollo's waitresses, especially Nelligan who, like Pfeiffer, manages to submerge her very attractive real-life appearance beneath the hard lines of an over-made-up, vulgar (but also warm-hearted) tart.

The (by now drearily familiar) rumours from the New York location for *Frankie and Johnny* were teaming Pfeiffer and Pacino as an item but she remained attached to Fisher Stevens and after filming was completed they spent a long vacation together in Europe.

Offers were pouring in, some for solid projects, some from wishful-thinkers. Pfeiffer turned down *Basic Instinct* which brought overnight notoriety to Sharon Stone (after the trauma of scene 105 the possibility of Pfeiffer accomplishing Stone's 'flash' is unthinkable), but didn't hesitate when she was offered the role of Catwoman in the sequel to the hugely popular *Batman*. It wasn't just the money – although a $3 million fee plus a percentage of the gross was surely tempting – but was also the chance to play a role with which she had been familiar since early childhood through the Batman comics and the 1960s television series.

Hollywood rumours had several actresses clawing and scratching at one another for the role and, for a while, the front-runners were apparently Annette Bening and Sean Young. Bening dropped out of the race when she and her husband, Warren Beatty, announced that she was pregnant.

As for Young, her aggressive eagerness to land the role seems to have frightened rather than impressed those who were planning the film.

In any event, the role went to Pfeiffer who promptly set about getting into super-fit shape for what would clearly be her most physically demanding role to date. She also had to learn how to use a bull-whip, something she achieved with remarkable dexterity.

Her principal trainer was womens' world champion kick boxer, Kathy Long, who also stood in for Pfeiffer on some of the many very athletic scenes including those involving climbing and the spectacular back flips.

Pfeiffer's co-star, reprising his role as Batman, was Michael Keaton and any worries either star, or the producers, might have had about bringing together the former lovers were quickly dispelled. They got along very well and neither found any embarrassment or difficulty in working together.

Batman Returns (1992) is a comparative rarity amongst sequels in that it improves upon the first-go-round by developing continuing characters instead of simply assuming that everyone has seen the first film and not only knew what to expect but also was prepared simply to accept the mixture as before. *Batman Returns* also manages, beneath the grotesqueries of appearance, dress and psyche of the comic-strip characters, to present people who have deep psychological problems which can be related to reality. The fact that some of them look like creatures from the animal kingdom is almost never obstructive.

A deformed infant is abandoned by his parents but lives to grow up in the sewers of Gotham City where his only friends are penguins. Many years later, now a grossly deformed adult, Oswald Cobblepot, known as the Penguin (Danny De Vito), returns as a frightening threat to the city and is behind a major crime wave that dismays citizens and their elected officials. The Penguin is also planning the wholesale murder of the city's first-born children in revenge for his treatment at the hands of his parents.

Desperate to rid Gotham of the curse, the Mayor and Police Commissioner Gordon (Michael Murphy and Pat Hingle) press the button which sends a message to the home of millionaire dilettante Bruce Wayne, who is secretly the masked crime-fighter, Batman (Keaton).

While down on the streets Batman begins to cleanse the city of the Penguin's gang of cut-throats, high above in the towering skyscrapers even more skulduggery is afoot. Millionaire businessman Max Shreck (Christopher Walken) is selling the Mayor the idea of a new power station which will supply all Gotham's electricity; except that the city doesn't need it.

Shreck's secretary, Selina Kyle (Pfeiffer), is a slightly frumpy, untidily disorganized young woman. She lives with her cat in a crowded apartment. A neon sign on the wall greets her every night when she comes home from the office: Hello There! Her answering machine is filled with messages; all from her mother.

When Selina discovers what her boss is up to she unwisely tells him that she knows. He off-handedly suggests a bribe but has something much more positive in mind and promptly pushes her through the window.

On the street, many floors down, as stray cats circle Selina's still body, she suddenly and amazingly stirs into life. Later that night, back in her apartment, Selina slashes her clothes, stuffs cuddly toys into the garbage disposal unit and then finds an old PVC skirt. This she transforms into a skin-tight garment which transforms her into a black-clad, masked, slinkily sensual and dangerous creature. She has become Catwoman.

During her trashing of her apartment, the neon sign has been damaged. Now its message is a warning: Hell here!

Meanwhile, the Penguin has emerged from the sewers to claim his real name and devote himself to good works. Rightly, Batman doesn't believe a word of this but the people respond to the Penguin's blandishments and he is joined by Shreck who offers to back him if he will run for Mayor and, if successful, ensure that the millionaire's unnecessary power-plant is built.

Batman, masked, attempts to foil the growing threat of Catwoman while Bruce Wayne, Batman unmasked, becomes attracted to the newly confident Selina Kyle.

Catwoman forms an uneasy alliance with the Penguin but when he kidnaps a beauty queen, the Ice Princess (Cristi Conaway), and then murders her, Catwoman becomes his enemy. The Penguin also tries to rid himself of Batman, first by attempting to frame him for the beauty queen's kidnap, then by sabotaging the Batmobile, Batman's state-of-the-art crime-fighting vehicle. Batman fights back and destroys the Penguin's chances at the forthcoming election by ensuring that the voters discover exactly what the would-be honest citizen really thinks of the people he would represent. Crazed with rage, the Penguin revives his homicidal plans and Gotham City's newly born infants are threatened.

Bruce and Selina have jointly realized that the other is the masked and mysterious night-time prowler. Selina offers the paw of friendship, saying, 'I hope this doesn't mean we have to fight.' Then the Penguin kidnaps Shreck's son, Chip (Andrew Brynlarski), but Shreck agrees to take his place. Beneath the city the Penguin sets loose a flock of penguins, each armed with a missile, but Batman comes to the rescue and the deadly birds are made to home on to the Penguin's lair and destroy it. The Penguin is killed and his body cast afloat in the sewers by a brood of his faithful followers.

At last face-to-face with Shreck, Catwoman takes her revenge for his attempt to kill Selina and electrocutes him. But the collapsing building traps her and she is buried with her victim.

Back in his mansion, Bruce Wayne reflects on what has happened. But all of Catwoman's nine lives have not been lost and across the city she reappears, silhouetted against the night sky.

For all the comic-strip silliness of things such as flocks of missile-carrying penguins, the manner in which screenwriter Daniel Waters and director Tim Burton explore the multiple instances of schizoid behaviour that pepper *Batman Returns* offers many fascinating moments. Bruce Wayne/Batman is a gloomy, reclusive, brooding figure, light-years away from the rather camp portrayal given by Adam West in the television series. This version of the caped crusader does what he does not as a night-time sport but because he is driven to his secret actions through inner forces over which he has no control. His faithful butler, Alfred (Michael Gough), constantly worries over his employer's behaviour in a manner which alters their relationship towards that of the master-monster partnerships which lie at the core of many classic horror films.

Oswald Cobblepot/Penguin is by turns a man tormented by betrayal and by the response to his deformities of everyone he meets. Through De Vito's layered performance the Penguin continually captures audience interest; first gaining sympathy and then replacing it with antipathy. Even after his final insanely homicidal behaviour, dregs of sympathy remain thus allowing the death scene to move audiences, but not to laughter.

Shreck is an exception to the split-personality theme, being presented as a deep-dyed villain with no redeeming features until close to the end when he takes his son's place as the Penguin's hostage. However, by making him an immensely rich man he is set up as a kind of alternative dark side to Bruce Wayne's rich philanthropist thus allowing the film's makers to show that money can be used for good and also to bring evil.

The split personality of Selina/Catwoman also offers an alternative view of the Bruce/Batman complex. Just as he adopts his guise to fight crime, something he cannot do as the slightly effete, coddled millionaire, she dons her cat-suit to revenge herself and womanhood in general against a host of slights, insults and assaults. Not that Catwoman is presented as a kind of goody-goody Wonder Woman. When, on her first appearance on Gotham's streets, Catwoman saves a woman from the clutches of a villainous male, she is bitterly contemptuous of the weak and watery victim – someone who is not a whole lot different from Selina herself in her pre-cat stage.

The psychological sides to the characters are clearly what interests Waters and Burton and some of the general action sequences are tossed away without much attention to detail. Burton's beginning in films was as an animator and this allowed him to explore his interest in the surreal and fantastic. Before *Batman* he made *Pee-Wee's Big Adventure* (1985) and *Beetlejuice* (1988), his first encounter with Michael Keaton. Between *Batman* and *Batman Returns* he made the surprisingly moving *Edward Scissorhands* (1990), which also explored the effects of deformity upon sufferer and onlookers.

If the general action sequences are sometimes left to themselves, Burton's attention to bizarre detail in all his work is often intense, perhaps echoing his animation origins although a spell at Disney was unproductive: 'I was sort of treated like the special retarded child.'

Highly imaginative details fill *Batman Returns*, especially in scenes featuring Catwoman. Pfeiffer's use of the potentially dangerous bull-whip is extremely well done, even allowing for the ability of the camera to deceive. Some of the fights, with Catwoman and Batman sliding up and down slippery rooftops (and occasionally and very sexily over one another) are also done well and confirm that Pfeiffer's hard work in getting herself in shape for the film was effort well spent. She also impressed the crew with her work on the scene in which Catwoman swallows the Penguin's pet canary. Pfeiffer unhesitatingly closed her mouth over the live bird in each of the twenty takes it took to get the scene right. She commented that her ability to control her reflexes meant that 'it wasn't really difficult'. (There are no reports of what the canary thought about it.)

In many ways this was a dream role for an actress. While the concept of a comic-strip character might seem inappropriate for a serious actress (it is impossible to think of Bette

Davis or Katharine Hepburn doing this kind of thing), the role allows Pfeiffer to show her versatility not only by making the shift from pre-fall dizzily disorganized Selina to post-fall confidently mature Catwoman, but also as the sexually wavering secretary to the provocative cat-suited all-action feline.

Pfeiffer also found that the script gave her some nice one-liners. When she is knocked off a rooftop by Batman she falls into a heavily laden open-topped truck, looks sideways at what she's fallen into, and remarks, 'Saved by Kitty-Litter'. When she looks out at the world for the first time as Catwoman, she murmurs, 'Life's a bitch, and so am I.'

Amongst the drawbacks to wearing skin-tight plastic when dressed in her cat-suit was the inevitable sweatiness and the wardrobe department had to come up with dozens of the suits so that when the discomfort became unbearable she could change into a fresh suit. The contour-revealing costume and the four-inch heels also attracted so much attention that she resorted to being driven around the set in a curtained golf cart.

Michael Keaton's experience on the first Batman film had warned him what to expect in trying to act through a suit of rubber and plastic. Gleefully, he awaited Pfeiffer's first day on the set. 'There she was, working her little heart out,' he told *Rolling Stone* magazine. 'The look on her face was totally committed but behind it was, "How did I get myself into this?" – the look of total fear!' However, he added, 'She's a *gamer*'.

She was also now in a very different Hollywood category. Gone were the days of being a B-list actress, now she had even surpassed the A-list. Amongst the advantages of the role of Catwoman, apart from the $3 million fee, was the fact that the film's massive success – it was the year's top grosser, pulling in $162.8 million – did what quality films like *Dangerous Liaisons* and *The Fabulous Baker Boys* could not do. They might have brought her the respect and admiration of her peers – to say nothing of two Academy Award nominations

– but *Batman Returns* made her not only bankable in her own right but also turned her into an internationally popular superstar.

7 *Hope and the End of a Dream*

The project in which Michelle Pfeiffer had been deeply involved just before making *Frankie and Johnny* was an interracial love story set against the background of the assassination of President John F. Kennedy in Dallas in November 1963.

Together with Kate Guinzburg, Pfeiffer had developed the project through their own production company. Although attitudes in Hollywood towards intimacy between blacks and whites had come a long way in the past decade, it was still an awkward topic for many to fully accept; certainly where money was concerned there was scepticism and nervousness.

In fact, the love story element is more hinted at than real, the depicted degree of intimacy a single short kiss (edited out when the film was shown in some places – and on some airlines). As Pfeiffer explained, what the film is really about is 'two people finding each other over one weekend and then changing each other's life drastically. It's the early sixties – the time of the suppression of black Americans and American women. It's about the liberation of these two people and the struggle for that liberation.'

Pfeiffer was set to co-star with Denzel Washington but he was uneasy from the start because he considered his role too passive (Washington had played Malcolm X in Spike Lee's film about the civil rights activist, a man who was anything but passive). Then, at the last moment, Washington pulled out. Adding to the tribulations of Pfeiffer-Guinzburg Productions, some studios offered backing but only if the relationship between the couple in the film could be rewritten so that they did not fall in love.

Pfeiffer was deeply shaken by Washington's decision: '. . . I felt like I had been broken up with. I felt I had been completely rejected.' As for requests to tone down the almost subliminal nature of the love story, she was furious: 'I was completely shocked. I wondered: "What century is this?" I mean, Jesus Christ, they've got people practically fucking each other on screen, and they've got people blowing each other's brains out. And here's this really sweet movie, and just because he happens to be black, and she happens to be white, everyone's afraid to make it.'

All of which shows that for all its claims and high hopes, and despite the presence of a new and vociferous wave of young black film-makers, Hollywood in the early 1990s has still to free itself from the deadening prejudices and bigotry that marred it for decades.

But for all the obstacles and disappointments, Pfeiffer never lost her enthusiasm nor her determination to see it through. Jonathan Kaplan was slated to direct and he confirmed that the problems only 'made her more resolved . . . She's someone who goes on instinct and if you tell her she can't do something, she'll want to do it twice as much.'

Well, Pfeiffer wanted to make *Love Field*, and this was exactly what she did, overcoming real and psychological hurdles in her determination to see the project through to completion.

Eventually, Pfeiffer-Guinzburg Productions won financial backing from Orion. Unfortunately, the problems didn't stop there. By the time the film was completed, at the end of 1991, Orion was in trouble. Unlike several film companies to hit financial difficulties, however, Orion under chairman John Kluge fought for survival and, after extensive restructuring, struggled back from bankruptcy. What was more, having survived, the company decided to use *Love Field* as the emblem of its victory. Everyone connected with the film was delighted, especially executive producers Pfeiffer, Guinzburg and George Goodman, and producers Sarah Pillsbury and Midge Sanford. The latter doubtless spoke for all with the declaration, 'It's a very surreal feeling. It's almost like a dream that people actually saw the film. It's been very frustrating especially in a town where it's "What have you done lately?", and what you've done lately is on a shelf somewhere.'

The film was premiered in December 1992, more than three years after Pfeiffer and Guinzburg had taken the project on board. The wait was worth it and Pfeiffer found herself nominated for the third time for an Academy Award, her second nomination as Best Actress.

The story of *Love Field* (1992) starts out in a simple, low-key manner. Lurene Hallett (Pfeiffer) lives in Dallas, Texas, with her husband, Ray (Brian Kerwin). Lurene is a hairdresser, living her life without expectancy of anything unusual or romantic. Theirs is an ordinary blue-collar existence; bowling, beer and television. But Lurene has an idol: Jackie Kennedy. And today, 22 November 1963, is a very special day in Lurene's life. Today, Jackie Kennedy and the President are coming to Dallas and Lurene, who has long admired the First Lady through magazines and television, will for the first time see her in the flesh.

The Kennedys are due to arrive in Dallas at Love Field, the airport in Richardson, a northern suburb of Dallas. Lurene will be taking the family car and as Ray is working and, anyway, isn't interested in the presidential visit, she has offered to take her wheelchair-bound neighbour, Mrs Heisenbuttel (Peggy Rea), along with her.

At Love Field, Lurene's moment draws closer when Jackie and the President walk across to the crowds of well-wishers to shake a few hands. But Mrs Heisenbuttel has dropped her handbag and by the time that Lurene has struggled through the crowd to retrieve it, then struggled back again, Jackie has moved on. To rub salt into Lurene's irritation, the First Lady actually shook hands with Mrs Heisenbuttel.

An hour or so later, as Lurene and her companion are

driving through Dallas, they notice people acting oddly, some are running, and police sirens everywhere are wailing. Climbing from the car, Lurene walks to a store window where she can see a television set and the newsflash breaking the shattering news. The President has been shot. A short while later, Lurene is at the hairdressing salon with her boss, Hazel (Beth Grant), her colleagues and their customers. Silently, they sit watching as the news broadcasts continue until, finally, Walter Cronkite announces that the President is dead.

Later that day, Lurene has made a decision; she will go to Washington for the funeral. She will be near her idol, Jackie, at a moment when she needs around her those that care. Lurene knows that she is being sentimental, that she will be nothing more than a face in the crowd. Ray doesn't hesitate in telling her what a fool she is, but Lurene is determined. In the evening, as Ray dozes in front of the television set, Lurene sneaks from the house, suitcase in hand, and heads for the bus depot.

The first leg of the journey is from Dallas to Memphis. Lurene is in the last row of the whites-only front section of the bus; just behind her, in the front seat of the back-of-the-bus section reserved for blacks, sits a man and a little girl. Lurene ingenuously introduces herself but the man is diffident, and the little girl completely withdrawn. But Lurene, garrulous to a fault, prattles on and eventually the man tells her his name is Paul Johnson (Dennis Haysbert) and the girl is his daughter, Jonell (Stephanie McFadden).

During the night, traffic is detoured through bad weather and the bus is involved in an accident with a speeding car which overtakes them, forcing the bus driver to swerve off the road. Most of the bus passengers are sleeping but Paul is awake and witnesses the accident but makes the mistake of telling Lurene he saw what happened. When police arrive, Lurene eagerly tells an officer that Paul saw everything and introduces him as Mr Johnson but Paul hastily tells the policeman that his name is Paul Cater. Lurene realizes that

Paul is obviously agitated at being pointed out to the police but for the moment says nothing.

At an enforced stop, Lurene offers to take Jonell into the ladies' washroom and while in there discovers that the little girl's body is a mass of bruises. Leaping to the conclusion that Paul is responsible, Lurene places a telephone call to the FBI in Dallas to inquire if there has been a report of a kidnapping, and telling them the payphone number she is calling from. Meanwhile, Paul is giving a statement about the accident to an antagonistic white cop but notices Lurene and Jonell and from the woman's behaviour intuitively guesses that something is amiss. Watched suspiciously by the cop, Paul tells Lurene the truth. His name really is Paul Cater, Jonell is his daughter, and, yes, he has kidnapped her; but only to rescue her from his ex-wife and her new husband who has been beating the little girl.

Lurene recognizes that Paul is telling her the truth but at that moment the payphone starts to ring and she knows that this will be the Dallas FBI calling her back. The three of them hurry from the depot just as the policeman Paul spoke to at the scene of the accident walks across and picks up the phone.

The police launch a search but Lurene and Jonell hide while Paul steals a car from a repair shop. Come daylight, they are on their way north but the car is going slower and slower – obviously this is a car that had yet to be fixed. When the car eventually grinds to a standstill, Lurene knows that they are close to where Hazel's mother lives. Convinced that her boss's mother will help them out, Lurene eagerly offers to hitch a ride for them, ignoring Paul's protestations that this is not a part of the country where a black man and a white woman travel together, let alone draw attention to themselves. Then a car slows down and a trio of rednecks survey them suspiciously before they speed off. A few minutes later, a small truck comes into view and Paul persuades Lurene to resume her journey to Washington alone. She agrees, reluctantly, and as the truck carrying her disappears up the road the first car reappears, heading slowly and menacingly towards the broken-down car. Paul tells his daughter to stay hidden in the car, whatever happens, before he walks up the road to meet the three men. Jonell watches as her father is badly beaten.

Meanwhile, Lurene has reached the house where Hazel's mother, Mrs Enright (Louise Latham), lives with her invalid husband. Lurene borrows a car from Mrs Enright, starts out north but then changes her mind and goes back to where she left Paul and Jonell. A short while later, Lurene returns to the Enright home with Paul and the little girl. Although reluctant to involve herself in what she can see is a potentially dangerous situation, Mrs Enright agrees to allow them to stay overnight. The little girl and Lurene can stay in the house, Paul will sleep in the barn. Then all of them are drawn to a television set as Lee Harvey Oswald, Kennedy's alleged assassin, is brought through the basement of the Dallas police station, only to be shot in front of the cameras.

That night, drawn together by their experiences, Lurene and Paul kiss in the barn. Next day, they leave in the Enrights' car with Lurene promising to return soon although Mrs Enright is clearly thankful that her unwelcome visitors have gone.

When the three travellers arrive in Washington, Lurene books into the motel where she and Ray spent their honeymoon. But Ray has guessed that this is where she is headed and is already there. Ray begins to beat up his wife and Paul intervenes; the two men fight and the police are called but Lurene, Paul and Jonell escape. Roadblocks around the area where the President's funeral cortège will pass trap them and, as Paul is arrested, Lurene runs away with Jonell. The police, believing that what is happening might be an attempt on the First Lady's life, surround them. Then, as Jonell is taken away and Lurene is being escorted into a police car, a limousine carrying Jackie Kennedy comes by and for the briefest of moments the eyes of the two women meet.

A year later, Lurene is divorced and regularly visits the

Dallas children's home where Jonell is living until her father is released from prison. One day, as Lurene leaves the home, Paul arrives and they greet one another cautiously before Lurene drives away. In Jonell's bedroom, father and daughter are reunited but then, through the window, Lurene's car comes back into view as she returns to the home.

Although the assassination of John Kennedy is the catalyst for the story of Lurene and Paul, it only rarely intrudes into the narrative in an overt manner. And yet, in a very real sense, the incident hovers over the couple like a cloud; much as the tragedy of that day in Dallas shadowed the lives of countless millions who had placed unreasoned, probably unreasonable and unrealistic hopes in Kennedy's presidency.

Lurene and Paul travel uncertainly and only gradually does her naïvety and guilessness give way to the realization that the world outside her narrow life is not at all the way she has imagined it to be. During her garrulous one-sided conversations with Paul she makes casual references to how much good the Kennedy administration has done for 'your people'. Only when he knows her a little better and they are in the black section of a small Southern town, trying to have the car fixed, does he tell her to look around and see for herself how much has really been done. She does so, and perhaps for the first time in her life sees things as they really are and not the way she has been told they are. It is a moment of learning, a moment when Lurene is forced into growing up, a moment when innocence ends.

Pfeiffer spoke of this when she compared the narrative of *Love Field* to how America responded to events in Dallas thirty years before the film was released. 'I think that I see a parallel in that Kennedy really represented a sense of hope for this country ... One of the parallels with *Love Field* is that it was period of a loss of innocence. The assassination of Kennedy was one of the biggest blows this country has ever suffered ... Even now it still moves people in such a primal way ... With Lurene there's a loss of innocence ...'

Sometimes, lost innocence can be interpreted in a negative manner; in Lurene's case it is the opposite. Until that day in Dallas, Lurene was self-centred, not maliciously or calculatedly so but simply because she had never taken the trouble, or felt the need, to stretch her mind. Now she does so, because some hitherto buried needs rise to the surface where they are joined by similarly suppressed unease at the nature of the society of which she has for so long been an unquestioning member. Who can say if Lurene will move on from there; but her decision to return to Paul's side is a brave one. It is one she may well regret in 1960s America. Whatever her future may hold, she will never again take anything for granted, nor will she accept things simply because this is the way they have always been.

The casting and performances in *Love Field* are near-perfect. Once again, Pfeiffer mastered an accent which is no mean feat given Lurene's non-stop chatter. She also looks the part with platinum-dyed hair in a style that looks armour-plated (and which appropriately changes to a softer natural look in the film's final sequence). Pfeiffer never allows a hint that Lurene's obsession with Jackie Kennedy is anything other than a harmless mooning over a role model. Neither does she make the mistake of allowing Lurene's awakening to take on mystical or intellectual overtones. She is simply a woman from whose eyes the scales have been lifted.

Apart from her playing with Haysbert, Pfeiffer's scenes with McFadden are extremely well done as the young girl responds to the talkative but kindly stranger, a woman unlike anyone she has ever met in her short and unhappy life.

Haysbert finds exactly the right note for his character at each stage of the journey. At first, he is uncomfortable with his prying fellow passenger simply because he has something to hide. To this is added growing uneasiness because she is white and they are moving literally into territory that is dangerous for him, in any event, and will become even worse if he involves himself with a white woman. Later, he begins to accept that Lurene's insistence on helping him and his daughter is prompted out of genuine kindness and is not in any way patronizing even if it is rooted in false beliefs about the status of blacks in Southern society. And then comes the slow dawning of the frightening discovery that he is falling in love across the racial divide. Indeed, the manner in which both principals handle this emotional transition is superbly realized.

As Pfeiffer asserted, Lurene is 'really a heroine. I think it is the willingness of both our characters to overcome boundaries, overcome race, overcome sex, overcome class that is a hopeful message . . . I think the film was about hope.'

For all the accomplishments of Pfeiffer, Haysbert and McFadden, it is Louise Latham, as elderly Mrs Enright, who leaves the strongest memory in the mind and with it the realization that the road to integration is one which stretches far into the past and probably, if depressingly, even farther into the future. Latham's face is frozen with tension, only her eyes reveal with painful accuracy the feelings of a woman who has lived in accordance with Southern attitudes on race for some seventy years but who has also been raised to be polite to strangers and those in distress, even to blacks although in their case with due distance and firmness. In addition, she may be intellectually aware that what she has been brought up to believe is wrong but she cannot abandon such deeply embedded prejudices. Lurene has to learn this today; Mrs Enright has known it all her life but has been obliged to bury the truth in order to survive.

All of the other supporting roles are done well, nowhere in the film is there a weak link in acting, direction, photography or editing.

The director, Jonathan Kaplan, has an interesting pedigree. Born in Paris, his father, Sol Kaplan, was blacklisted during the Hollywood House Committee on Un-American Activities witchhunt. A protégé of Martin Scorcese, Kaplan made a number of exploitation films for Roger Corman, then drifted in-and-out of the mainstream. These shifts mostly resulted from his refusal to repress his radical instincts for

too long and his habitual disregard for the commercial ne-
cessities that surround film-making in Hollywood. His films
include *Over the Edge* (1979), *Heart Like a Wheel* (1983) and *The
Accused* (1983), for which Jodie Foster won the Oscar as Best
Actress.

Despite the fact that in late 1993 *Love Field* sidled quietly
on to the video market in Britain, where it did not go on
general theatrical release, it is clear from Pfeiffer's observa-
tions at the time of its American release, and later, that she
regards the film as one of the most important and best she
has made. It is a point of view which is impossible to contradict. Curiously enough, the fact that *Love Field* didn't have a
theatrical release in Britain was seen by one critic, Julie
Birchill, as a sign of Pfeiffer's decline as a box-office attraction. In an article (on Julia Roberts) in *The Sunday Times* in
February 1994, Birchill remarked, 'So tired is the audience
judged to be of the beautiful and brilliant Michelle Pfeiffer
that one of her recent films, *Love Field*, was not even released
in European cinemas.'

A point of view, certainly, but one that is open to question.
Perhaps a reason for the lack of interest shown by distribu-
tors is hinted at in an article by Peter Millar which, coincidentally, appeared in the same issue of the newspaper. In
this, Millar recounted how a nineteen-year-old woman had
been to see a London screening of Oliver Stone's *JFK* and
remarked, 'That was a great film, and apparently it was
based on something that really happened.' Hard though it
might be for some people to accept, those events in Dallas
which are seared on to the memories of millions are either
forgotten or even unknown history to the new film-going
generation.

Whatever the reason for British and European lack of
interest, *Love Field* is a film of which Pfeiffer-Guinzburg
Productions can be very proud.

For her role as Lurene Hallett, Pfeiffer was nominated for
a Best Actress Oscar (as was Susan Sarandon for *Lorenzo's
Oil*, a film Pfeiffer had turned down) but the name that came

out of the envelope on the big night was that of Emma Thompson for *Howard's End*.

Failure to win the Oscar was more than compensated for by changes in Pfeiffer's private life. During the previous year, 1992, her relationship with Fisher Stevens had come to an end. The difficulties imposed by her residence in California and his three thousand miles away on the opposite coast had magnified. She wanted a different sort of life to the three-weeks-together, three-weeks-apart kind she endured with Stevens. She wanted something more settled; close friends said she craved domesticity. They came to a parting of the ways with some measure of amicability although the press picked up a story which hinted openly, but as usual with such things without real evidence, that Stevens had been spending time with an extra on a film he was making in North Carolina. By the time Stevens had moved on to another location, this time in Florida where he was working on a television series, the relationship with Pfeiffer was at an end.

Pfeiffer was philosophical about the split: 'People have a lot of relationships – they're not all meant to last a lifetime ... The truth is there are very few people in your life who are your soulmate.'

When *Love Field* was premiered in December 1992, Pfeiffer attended with David Kelley, a former lawyer who had entered television as co-creator of *LA Law* and had gone on to produce and co-write other television series, such as *Doogie Howser MD* and *Picket Fences*. Pfeiffer was cautious about her new companion, declaring that this was 'the most grown-up relationship I've had'. She was certainly maturely confident in herself. 'I think I was in a very good place before I met David ... I guess basically in my life I don't know that I would change anything.'

But before she began dating Kelley, she had decided upon a change which was to have a profound effect upon her private life.

She had begun to feel the need for a child and had secretly opened negotiations to adopt a baby girl. She did not consider that this was something for which she needed a permanent man in her life. 'Roles have changed so radically we don't know any longer how men are supposed to be, or how women are supposed to be. It's up to individuals to define their own rules.'

The baby, a girl named Claudia Rose, was born on the east coast on 5 March 1993. The mother was reportedly a woman of forty, already the mother of four, who runs a home nursing-care service. Adoption arrangements were made privately through lawyers, with Pfeiffer and the natural mother meeting during the pregnancy. Independent arrangements such as this allow the participants freedom to confirm their decisions after the birth of the child and the person making the adoption pays only the natural mother's medical expenses.

The day after the birth, Pfeiffer flew back to Los Angeles with Claudia Rose in a specially-chartered private airplane. Claudia Rose promptly became the centre of the actress's life. Pfeiffer chose not to hire live-in help, believing that it was necessary for her to become as close as possible to the child and that hiring staff would create unhelpful barriers.

As she told Leslie Bennetts in *Vanity Fair*, 'I had been ready to be a mother for a very long time . . . I thought about all my options, and certainly one of those options was to just have a baby with somebody, which I guess is the obvious option. But when it came right down to it, I just couldn't do it. I thought, I don't want some guy in my life forever who's going to be driving me nuts.'

But, however devoted she is to Claudia Rose, and about that there is clearly no doubt, it was still necessary for her to work and the film on which she had been most recently working was an important step not only for her but also for its director, Martin Scorsese, and, in many respects, for the re-emergence of maturity in American mainstream cinema after decades of reliance upon violence, action, sex, fantasy, hardware and special effects.

The film which marked a possible turnaround was an adaptation for the screen of a classic American novel, written in the 1920s and set in late nineteenth-century New York City.

The work of Henry James had tantalizingly offered excellent characterizations and intense explorations of manners and mores in nineteenth-century Boston and New York and amongst Americans living abroad (James himself ended his life in England, becoming a British citizen a year before his death in 1916). The solidity of James's prose style was a problem which countered many of his merits; much of it took some digesting if it was to be refashioned in any other terms apart from the long complex novels he favoured. When Michelle Pfeiffer chose drama classes at Fountain Valley High School in order to avoid having to write essays about Henry James she was acknowledging a problem others had already faced and frequently failed to surmount. Nevertheless, even in failure some good films still emerged, for example *The Heiress* (1949) which was based upon a stage play adaptation of James's *Washington Square*. The redoubtable non-Hollywood team of Merchant-Ivory-Prawer Jhabvala fared quite well with *The Europeans* (1979) but even they didn't refine *The Bostonians* (1984) sufficiently to allow the light to gleam through.

Perhaps it was fear of writers in the Henry James mode, perhaps it was simply an oversight, but another American writer of enormous distinction remained little touched by Hollywood until the early 1990s when she suddenly became a hot literary property. This was Edith Wharton, almost forgotten in the years following her death. The life she led, and the books she wrote prove her to have been a woman of distinction and a novelist with uncommon gifts. It is not surprising, therefore, that Michelle Pfeiffer would become fascinated by her. Separated by a century though they are, certain parallels may be observed in the attitudes of the two women, accentuated, perhaps, by the fact that in many ways Edith Wharton was a woman out of her time.

Born Edith Newbold Jones, in New York City, on 24 January 1862, she grew up in privileged circumstances. Her family was one of New York's Top Four Hundred and she was thus well-placed to observe the complacent world of which she would later become a chronicler, writing with often painful accuracy of that society's failings.

New York's top people set high standards for themselves which influenced their personal and business lives. In her memoirs, Edith Wharton would refer to their 'scrupulous probity' in all things. Her setting for *The Age of Innocence* is New York in the 1870s. She herself had lived in Chelsea, a district of brownstones and brick town houses inhabited by the likes of financier Jay Gould and Tammany Hall's Boss Tweed. It is a neighbourhood which would later go into steep decline but in her day, and the days in which the story is set, it was a very superior address. The people with whom Wharton's family and friends moved included some of the most famous names in America, not least the Rockefellers.

When she wrote *The Age of Innocence*, Wharton was living in France where she had moved before the First World War. The novel was published in 1921 and with it she became the first woman to be awarded a Pulitzer Prize. She stayed in France, where she wrote several more novels before her death on 11 August 1937.

Considering the background of the novelist and her novel, at first glance it might seem unusual that it should be Martin Scorcese who chose to develop *The Age of Innocence* as a film for the 1990s. Such a glance would range over striking examples of tough and often bloody encounters in what were usually very much male-dominated films. However, introduced to Wharton's novel by Jay Cocks, with whom he would collaborate on the screenplay, Scorcese discovered elements with which he could empathize, notably the strength of family ties and the ferocity with which this element of society defends itself. Scorcese was ready to make comparisons with other societies with which he has been associated in past films: 'Wharton describes almost like an anthropologist the rituals and mores of that society. In a way, they are like the rules of the mafia, and I find that fascinating.' Like the mafia, those who break the rules by which their peers live are targeted for destruction in order that this society will be protected from the dangers within and thus better able to maintain a solid front against the dangers without.

As Cocks observed, *The Age of Innocence* is 'not dramatic in action, but there are other kinds of drama. You don't always need a gun . . . [Wharton] had a moralist's vision and an ironist's vision. She knew how lethal the social machine was.'

Cocks had asked Scorcese to read the novel as long ago as 1980 but he failed to do so until some seven years later. When he did so, the aspect of Wharton's work which most attracted him was the love story element, 'that sense of an incredible passion without consummation, which becomes exquisitely painful. I wanted to explore that . . .'

He was also intrigued by the violence of the behaviour of the characters; *emotional* violence, not the physical kind with which he had been previously linked in the minds of audiences and Hollywood's money men, with whom the director has not always had an easy time.

After working independently in New York, as an editor, writer and director, Scorcese was hired by Roger Corman to make *Boxcar Bertha* (1972). The following year he had an unexpected success with *Mean Streets* and was then invited to make *Alice Doesn't Live Here Anymore* (1974) before bursting upon the general consciousness with the explosive *Taxi Driver* (1975). An up-and-down period followed with mixed critical and financial fortunes befalling *New York, New York* (1977), *Raging Bull* (1980), *The King of Comedy* (1982) and *After Hours* (1985). Scorcese had wanted to make *The Last Temptation of Christ* but the studio behind the project developed cold feet at the last moment, fearing a backlash from religious fundamentalists. Scorcese continued to move in and out of the mainstream with *The Color of Money* (1986), *The Last Temptation of Christ* (which eventually was made and appeared in 1988), *GoodFellas* (1989) and *Cape Fear* (1991), which was a huge box-office hit although Scorcese was unimpressed with the work. A remake of the 1962 film, *Cape Fear* was necessarily impersonal and that is something his best work has never been.

Highly personal, and a key to understanding his work, is Scorcese's fascination with New York society at many levels. In particular he is drawn to the nature of longing, of obsessive behaviour, and of violence both physical and emotional, all of which run like matching if not continuing threads through his best work: *Mean Streets, Taxi Driver, Raging Bull, GoodFellas.* Seen in this broad, developing and constantly maturing context, and recognizing also that one of the first films to make an impression on him as a child was *The Heiress*, the attraction for Scorcese of Edith Wharton's novel becomes much less surprising. Scorcese's interest, and the remarkable care, attention to detail, and love he lavished upon the production of *The Age of Innocence* not only restored Wharton to her rightful place in the history of classic American literature, it also ensured that the director, already a name recognized and admired by critics, film buffs, and his peers, should now be enshrined as one of the immutable icons of classic American cinema.

8   *Innocent Shadows of Reality*

Martin Scorcese had seen and been deeply impressed by Michelle Pfeiffer's acting ability, and wanted her for the role of Ellen Olenska in his planned adaptation to the screen of Edith Wharton's novel, *The Age of Innocence*. 'The thing that really clinched it,' Scorcese said, 'was *Married to the Mob*. She had a kind of honesty of character . . . She really was like the people I grew up with . . . and here was an actress of a different type, different background, coming in and making me believe totally. That really made me sit up and take note. And then, when *Dangerous Liaisons* came out, I thought, "She's the best we have."'

When he began casting *The Age of Innocence* (1993), Scorcese wanted Daniel Day-Lewis as Newland Archer in addition to choosing several other British actors and actresses. This was in recognition of that aspect of the people in the story who strove to be even more English than the English in their desire to cling to past values in a rapidly changing world. In the role of May Welland, Scorcese cast the rising young American actress, Winona Ryder.

The story begins when Newland first sees Ellen at the opera; significantly, it is a performance of *Faust*, a tale of repressed passion, obsession and, ultimately, the loss of a man's soul. Newland is about to become engaged to May; both are members of suitable families and are in love although he has had a previous romantic relationship. But Newland is not fully at ease with his impending marriage to May. As Wharton writes: 'With a new sense of awe he looked at the frank forehead, serious eyes and gay innocent mouth of the young creature whose soul's custodian he was to be

... and once more it was borne in on him that marriage was not the safe anchorage he had been taught to think.'

Ellen Olenska, formerly Ellen Mingott, is May's cousin. She is recently returned from Europe where her marriage to a Polish Count, Stanislas Olenski, is in difficulties. Ellen is very different from May and indeed from all the other women Newland has met. Her time in Europe has given her a different attitude towards others, towards herself, and about her role in life. This is no veneer but a deep and real understanding of herself and the position to which she might aspire in life but which the hidebound society of New York's upper set will not permit.

Ellen is welcomed cautiously. Her marriage to a foreigner made her suspect; her separation tars her. But for all their diffidence, the family protects her and aids her financially; for all her apparent waywardness, she is one of their own. Her grandmother, the formidable matriarch of the clan, Mrs Manson Mingott (Miriam Margolyes), supports her in many ways, and she and Newland persuade one of the city's best families, the Van der Luydens (Michael Gough and Alexis Smith), to acknowledge Ellen. But Ellen cannot ever be completely accepted back into the tight circle of which she was a part through birth but which, from choice, she has chosen to desert. There are even hints that her moral standards might be less than theirs. The philandering Count Olenski is undoubtedly the guilty party in their failed marriage but fail it did and she is tainted by that failure. And, perhaps, she might have sought consolation with a man since then. Whatever the truth, Ellen no longer fulfills the criteria, of blamelessness and probity in all things, that this section of New York society rigorously demands. Newland becomes steadily drawn to Ellen and she to him but the social barriers appear insurmountable; his feelings, however, do not escape the eagle-eyed Mrs Mingott nor, indeed, the 'serious eyes' of his fiancée.

Newland and May are married but he cannot overcome his attraction to Ellen and travels to Boston where she has gone to visit friends. There, he meets Monsieur Rivière (Jonathan Pryce), the Count's secretary, who carries entreaties from Olenski that Ellen return to him. She refuses, an action which can only confirm the family's fears that her standards are not theirs. As her grandmother says, 'I know my Ellen – haughty, intractable; shall I say, just a shade unforgiving?'

Newland is encouraged in his belief that Ellen is a special person by Rivière who confides in him that although he came to America certain that it was right and proper for Ellen to return to the Count he no longer holds that opinion. 'After I had seen her, after I had listened to her, I knew she was better off here.' He tells Newland that he had never before thought of her as an American and how that made a difference. 'If you're an American of *her* kind – of your kind – things that are accepted in certain other societies, or at least put up with as part of a general convenient give-and-take – become unthinkable, simply unthinkable.' But Rivière has misjudged the clannishness and rigidity of the Mingotts and their kind; there is no give-and-take here, certainly not for a woman.

Newland tells Ellen about the small-minded views of the New York set when he, of all people, is urged by the family to advise her on whether or not she should divorce the Count. 'We're damnably dull. We've no character, no colour, no variety. I wonder why you don't go back?'

For a long moment she is silent, then she tells him, 'I believe it's because of you.' Continuing, she explains how he has helped her understand that beneath the surface are 'things so fine and sensitive and delicate that even those I most cared for in my other life look cheap in comparison.'

Ellen decides that she will not return to her husband and the family withdraws some of its financial assistance. With no more money coming from the Count, Ellen's position worsens when she loses her investments through the bankruptcy of her financial adviser, Julius Beaufort (Stuart Wilson), a womanizer of whom Newland is needlessly jealous. But Ellen and Newland are no longer in doubt about their

In from the cold: 'Katya', an unwilling spy in *The Russia House*

Cold war games: 'Katya' in Red Square with Sean Connery in
The Russia House

Everything's off: weary waitresses 'Frankie' and Kate Nelligan
in *Frankie and Johnny*

Canary-yellow-alert: 'Catwoman' and bull-whip in *Batman Returns*

Bat-catted: 'Catwoman' proving she's top-dog to Michael Keaton in *Batman returns*

After Dallas: an end to innocence for 'Lurene' in *Love Field* with Stephanie McFadden and Dennis Haysbert

Love and hypocrisy: 'Ellen' and Daniel Day-Lewis held apart by unbreachable social barriers in *The Age of Innocence*

A different kind of woman: 'Countess Ellen Olenska' in *The Age of Innocence*

A hurtful secret love: 'Ellen' and Daniel Day-Lewis share a rare moment of privacy in *The Age of Innocence*

Casually tangled, the open-air California girl gleams through
this habitual defensive pose

Elaborately tangled, the sophisticatedly cool young woman of
the world is still defensively posed

feelings for one another and however much they try to step back, they are pulled irresistibly together again. As Newland tells her, 'Each time you happen to me all over again.'

Their secret love is hurtful to them both. Ellen tells him: 'If you're not blind, then, you must see that this can't last.'

'What can't?'

'Our being together – and not together.'

If they cannot become accepted as man and wife, she asks him if he wants her as his mistress; but he dreams of them being together in a world where they can live as 'two human beings who love each other, who are the whole of life to each other; and nothing else on earth will matter.'

But this is only a dream, an unrealistic hope which Ellen knows can never be fulfilled. Her fears that she and Newland will never be together appear to be confirmed when May tells her that she is pregnant by Newland. Ellen knows that now she has no choice but to return to Europe. She makes her plans, unaware that May is not yet sure about her claim of pregnancy and has, anyway, said nothing of this to Newland.

As pressures mount against Newland he is helpless to resist; if he protests too much then May will know the truth about his feelings for her and for Ellen. And this would serve only to betray Ellen and confirm the opinions the family has about her suspected moral laxity. So he says nothing, does nothing, and thus ends forever any chance of the two lovers finding happiness with one another.

For Newland this is not merely the loss of the woman he truly loves, but subjugation to May who has grown in strength as she moves towards becoming the new matriarch of the clan – a formidable replacement of the ailing Mrs Mingott.

Newland and Ellen, the true lovers – despite the fact that their passion remains unconsummated – and May, who recognizes that in victory she is defeated, reconcile themselves to lives without love.

Twenty-six years later, May is dead and Newland, now fifty-seven, visits Paris with his son, Ted (Robert Sean

Leonard), one of his three children. Ellen lives in Paris and they bear greetings from the family who have held her in fond regard ever since she left their midst and thus ceased to be a danger to them. Ted (named Dallas in the novel) tells his father that the day before May died she told him that she knew the children would be safe with their father, 'and always would be, because once, when she asked you to, you'd given up the thing you most wanted.'

But that is not how it happened. 'She never asked me,' Newland says.

Newland and Ted go to the apartment building where Ellen lives but only the young man goes up to pay the family's respects to their distant and distanced relative. Newland sits alone in the courtyard beneath Ellen's window.

'It's more real to me here than if I went up,' he says aloud.

He must acknowledge that fear 'lest that last shadow of reality should lose its edge kept him rooted to his seat as the minutes succeeded each other.'

When Edith Wharton wrote The *Age of Innocence* she was exhausted by her work and experiences in wartime France. In writing it, she later said, 'I found an escape in going back to my memories of a long-vanished America.' Clearly, there is more than this in *The Age of Innocence*. Whether or not it was exhaustion, or the surge of an emotional tide, there is more of the writer in this tale than in any of her other novels. Parallels with her own life abound. Mostly through Newland Archer (who is the novel's dominant figure – indeed, the writer chooses never to enter Ellen's mind), glimpses of Wharton's own passions and frustrations emerge. She was fifty-seven when she wrote the book, the age Newland is when he sits outside Ellen's window; and Ellen is isolated in Paris far from her original roots, just as was Wharton. Newland endured his loveless marriage for twenty-six years; Wharton's marriage to Teddy Robbins Wharton was a mistake she suffered for twenty-eight years. Some of Wharton's frustrated passions were released through her affair with journalist Morton Fullerton; a release Newland and Ellen could not enjoy except in their imaginations as they failed to surmount obstacles constructed to keep them apart.

There are other features which reflect Wharton's life and yet, astonishingly, given its emotional depth and subtleties, its perception and riches, *The Age of Innocence* was not written to deliberately exorcize Wharton's pent-up emotional demons; it was written in haste because she needed the money (her own money was tied up in America and was for some time inaccessible due to the after-effects of the war in Europe), and it was first published unceremoniously in a magazine. For all this, as Penelope Lively summarized it in her introduction to the Virago Press edition of *The Age of Innocence*; the novel is a 'rich and powerful description of a vanished world, alternately witty and moving, presenting with marvellous control and range a group of characters who between them define a whole period and culture.' But it is not a simplistic world. As Wharton herself observes in the novel, its inhabitants 'all lived in a hieroglyphic world, where the real thing was never said or done or even thought, but only represented by a set of arbitrary signs.'

In his approach to filming this vanished cryptic world, director Scorcese drew inspiration primarily from the novel but also from outside sources, amongst them the manner in which Luchino Visconti created the appearance and atmosphere of the Italian *risorgimiento* in *The Leopard* (1963). Scorcese screened the film for his cast and technicians, using the lovingly restored version not that which was foisted on to the public outside Italy by unimaginative vandals at the studio which first released the film in the USA. Scorcese's cinematographer, German-born Michael Ballhaus, tellingly explores the vanished opulence of New York in the 1870s, recreated for the film by production designer Dante Ferretti, just as did Giuseppe Rotunno for Visconti's portrayal of that other vanished world.

Scorcese also recognized the value of Wharton's words in the novel, sometimes gently persuasive, at other times lightly sardonic, and uses them selectively in voice-over narration (by Joanna Woodward).

With firm sensitivity, Scorcese guides his actors through a recreation of a world which none had known but which, thanks to his empathy with the novelist, all are able to infuse with sympathy and understanding. In particular, Scorcese uses dinner scenes – eight of them – to heighten the impression of order and control. Every piece of the dinner service, every place setting, every fork or knife, is a visual symbol of the invisible building blocks in the impregnable structure which surrounds the characters and which helps foil Newland Archer in his hopeless attempts to breach the walls. As Scorcese pointed out to Ian Christie in *Sight and Sound*, ' . . . when the Van der Luydens create a dinner for Countess Olenska, they are making a statement and daring people to go against them.'

With his off-camera colleagues in full accord with his vision – Cocks, Ballhaus, Ferretti and, especially, his long-time associate, editor Thelma Schoonmaker – Scorcese succeeds in bringing to vivid life an era of American cultural history not so much forgotten as never really remembered since Edith Wharton's novels fell into obscurity. He also met the challenge of bringing to the camera the repressed passion experienced by Newland and Ellen through their unconsummated love – miraculously turning a scene where Newland unbuttons Ellen's glove and gently kisses her wrist into one of the most sexually charged moments in film history.

The director and his editor (who won an Oscar for her work on *Raging Bull*) benefited from a decision by the studio to extend the post-production schedule. For Scorcese and Schoonmaker, both of whom believe that the editing room is where the real film-making begins, the extra nine months they were given allowed them to fully realize their original objectives.

Scorcese's cast rose magnificently to the challenge of breathing life into their characters. Miriam Margolyes exudes the diamond-sharpness of the Mingott matriarch who controls many of the family's actions in her ultimately doomed attempt to sustain a way of life already slipping away through its introspection and inbred decadence. There are impeccable performances from a remarkable roster of supporting and character actors including Gough, Smith, Pryce, Wilson, Richard E. Grant, as the egregious Larry Lefferts, and Sîan Phillips, as Mrs Archer.

The three principals, Day-Lewis, Pfeiffer and Ryder are similarly flawless. Winona Ryder gives May perfect attributes, what *The European*'s critic, Richard Mayne, called 'steely frailty' and slips skilfully beneath the skin of a woman who is not intellectually gifted but is filled with a kind of intelligence that constantly outwits those who believe themselves to be her superiors. As Newland says of her, she can never be emancipated because she has 'not the dimmest notion that she was not free' but then the extent of his misjudgement is revealed by her 'instinctive guile' which she employs to bend her fiancé to her will. It is no easy task to convey the behaviour of a character who, on the surface, is a wronged woman, virtuous and the epitome of the honest, righteous people who make up her social set, yet underlying this are hints that she wants marriage to Newland not out of love but through a need for stability and station even if it means robbing him, and Ellen, of any chance of happiness. Ryder deftly portrays these ambiguities, never making May appear malicious and concealing her intrigues beneath the surface calm of considerable physical beauty.

Daniel Day-Lewis clearly knew that his was a dream role. Newland Archer is one of the screen's most complex protagonists of recent years. He cannot be accurately termed a hero because he is deeply flawed with so many potentially catastrophic weaknesses. He is a bored dilettante, he is deeply affectionate towards his fiancée yet indifferent to her and dismissive of her needs. An idle, rich man who plays at being a lawyer, he cannot view his own life with the necessary judicious detachment. He is desperate in his love for Ellen, yet afraid to reveal to his peers the depths of his emotional entanglement. And, ultimately, he is afraid to flout the rules created by his own society for its members' protection. He must therefore live out his days in solitary confinement in a prison he has helped construct.

With enormous skill and seemingly effortless ease, Day-Lewis achieves all of these complex, conflicting and shifting aspects of his character's troubled existence. As he said of his character, Newland Archer is at ease with his background and surroundings ' . . . but also at the same time in his imagination, in the reality of his life, he's stretching beyond that world which is, in fact, a suffocating one . . . he dreams of perhaps going beyond the frontiers of that environment but at the same time he's very much a part of it.'

The character of Ellen Olenska is one which offered Michelle Pfeiffer an opportunity to explore the nature of a woman who, like Pfeiffer herself, and Edith Wharton, was not afraid to resist the pressures of a society which made its rules in an attempt at self-preservation. Women who succeeded in Wharton's world, both real and in her fiction, and women who were able to do so for many years in Pfeiffer's world, were obliged to play to the rules laid down for them by men. Wharton broke the rules and won. Her Ellen Olenska broke the rules and, while she might appear to have gone down in defeat to entrenched hypocrisies, she emerged as a mirror image of May, the victor who lost. Ellen lost, but was nevertheless left to live out her life on her own terms. Pfeiffer, too, has succeeded, first by playing to the rules until she was powerful, then by helping other modern women in Hollywood to make new rules and win by them, too.

Given such a confluence of similarities of character and the worlds in which they separately existed, it is not surprising that Pfeiffer brings to her portrayal of Wharton's embattled heroine great depths of understanding. She gives Ellen at once an alluringly sophisticated other-worldliness and a softly vulnerable charm that makes it easy to understand Newland Archer's helplessness and the headlong dash he makes towards a hopelessly unattainable dream.

'It was an impossibility,' Pfeiffer said of the love between Ellen and Newland, 'not because it was a fantasy in their minds and because the love wasn't real but I think that the guilt would have destroyed any kind of love, any kind of chance that they may have had. It would have just over-ridden them.'

Unusually, for someone so highly self-critical, Pfeiffer expressed pleasure in her interpretation. 'I was happy with the performance, and that's unusual for me. I'm never pleased with an entire performance. It's percentages with me, and the last time I saw *The Age of Innocence*, it had the highest percentages. This was a difficult, different part. The dialogue ran the risk of being arch. You wanted to colloquialize but you couldn't be too contemporary either, so there was a fine line.'

Everyone connected with *The Age of Innocence* had complete justification in feeling satisfied with their work and pride in the finished product. To this could be added the critical acclaim with which the film was greeted in America, where it was released in September 1993, and throughout Europe where it was shown during the following months. Some critics diluted their praise a little, feeling that the film did not fully capture Wharton's ironic tone. In this context, *Ethan Frome* (1993), starring Liam Neeson and Patricia Arquette, filmed from another Wharton novel, fared rather better even if it was allowed to slip almost unnoticed on to the art-house circuit.

The Age of Innocence also met with considerable financial success everywhere it was shown, a fact which will hopefully have given pause to those who believe that box-office profitability is directly linked to nothing other than sex and action, the qualities most apparent in many latter-day blockbusters.

There was still the hoped-for recognition by the Hollywood peers of the actors, actresses and crew who had worked on the film. Would they, or wouldn't they, be nominated for Academy Awards? The nominations for the 1993

Oscars were preceded by months of speculation. That is not unusual. But in this year one film in particular was attracting a great deal of attention. Heavily touted as an odds-on favourite for nomination in several categories, including the 'big four' – Best Film, Best Director, Best Actor and Best Actress – was *The Age of Innocence*. If a nomination for Pfeiffer, as Best Actress, were to come it would be at a crossroads in her life and career. Her personal circumstances were changing and her career looked to be taking second place behind her life as a mother. This, added to her dismay at the perpetual invasion of privacy that clouded her life, might be prompting changes. Still deeply interested in and committed to films and film-making, the future might see her more involved behind the scenes and it just might be that opportunities for Oscars for on-screen activities will become less frequent in the future.

Coincidentally, however, just as Michelle Pfeiffer had other, more important, things on her mind at the time of her nomination for Best Actress for *Love Field*, so, too, was she preoccupied in the early months of 1994. Even more striking – and something no Hollywood scriptwriter would have dared suggest – was the fact that her preoccupation was of a very similar nature. Last time, she had just adopted Claudia Rose. This time, she had just learned that she was pregnant.

9   The Price of Privacy

As 1993 drew towards its close, Michelle Pfeiffer's career and private life were both in excellent shape. The occasional uncertainties of her work in the distant past had been completely overwhelmed by the towering, yet curiously understated, confidence she displayed in everything she touched since the breakthrough year of 1988/9. It was then that *Married to the Mob, Dangerous Liaisons* and *The Fabulous Baker Boys* tumbled out of the studios in quick succession, startling the motion-picture industry and the popular audience with her audacious versatility, acting skills, panache and sheer *class*.

Some time ago, Richard Corliss, in *Film Comment*, summed up her status when he wrote: 'So far, Pfeiffer has been called upon to project an attitude rather than to be an Actress. No suicide scenes, no hysterical phone calls; she has not once given birth or died of a TV-movie disease. That's fine. She has done more. She has shown how the notion of elegance can accommodate itself to the California decades of this century, and suggested, with wit and sleek style, how it might survive into the next.'

Pfeiffer herself is remarkably disingenuous about her achievements: 'Every time I do a movie, I think this is the one where they're going to find me out, that I'm a total and utter fraud. And every time I get to say to myself, "Well, Michelle, you got away with it again." '

Nevertheless, however she might reflect upon the hazards of a career in an industry with more than its share of broken dreams and unfulfilled promise, she had reached a stage where there was no longer any need to look back. She could, instead, concentrate upon the future. But there was never any hint that she would do so without caution.

Her upbringing was partially responsible for her attitude towards any business dealings she might have. 'My father . . . would say things like, "Trust everyone, Shel – but cut the cards." '

In an industry noted for underhand actions and knife-in the-back wheeling and dealing in which probity comes well after profitability in an upside-down lexicon, it has proved to be very useful advice.

Similarly useful has been another of her qualities: 'My greatest asset and my greatest curse is that I'm so fucking self-sufficient. I've always been impatient with myself. I've always wanted everything yesterday. My basic nature is dark. I alternate between candour and distrust.'

Alternative aspects of human psychology such as these expressed by Pfeiffer have long proved fascinating to film-makers. Nowhere have they been as overtly depicted as in a curious aspect of myth and legend that has attracted Holly-wood for decades and which was approached, yet again, in a Pfeiffer film that was already in the can. Although man-made monsters make their appearance with monotonous and frequently predictable, boring regularity, the fear of psychological deviation has exercised a strong grip on imagi-nations. Most popular amongst these, until the latter-day advent of the psychotic killer (from Norman Bates to Hanni-bal Lecter) have been men who are not only split in mind and personality but are also divided in their outward form; vam-pires and werewolves.

The legend of the werewolf centres upon a man (usually) who, on being bitten by a particular kind of wolf and living to tell the tale – and to regret the experience – finds himself undergoing psychological and physiological change. The subject came in for big-budget, star-studded treatment with *Wolf* (1994), a film which had the cachet absent in many of its B-movie predecessors of being made by a director who is customarily associated with very different genres.

Mike Nichols is a brilliantly gifted individual with a string of Broadway successes but a somewhat variable career as a film director. *Wolf* stars Jack Nicholson as Will Randall, an anti-social book editor, whose psychological problems explode with a vengeance after he is bitten by a young wolf. In this version of the ancient legend, however, the wolf-man is on the side of the righteous. Thanks to his change of character, Will is able to save his prestigious employers from an unscrupulous millionaire, Richard Alden (Christopher Plummer), who is aided by Will's duplicitous friend, Stewart Swinton (James Spader). Will has also been having problems with his adulterous wife, Charlotte (Kate Nelligan), but he now finds an ally in Alden's daughter, Laura (Pfeiffer), who hates her father and wants him to be defeated in his latest venture.

A literate script and good performances help the film, as do clever special effects (by Rick Baker, who performed more spectacular wonders in the 1981 film, *An American Werewolf in London*). The overall effect is interesting (what would happen to a publishing company if its comfortably middle-aged, pipe-smoking editor turned into a wolf?) but just a mite contrived. Pfeiffer described the film, a little uncertainly, as 'kind of a romantic-comedy-thriller. Sort of.'

The film ran into casting problems during its pre-production phase. Sharon Stone was originally lined up for the role taken by Pfeiffer; and Nelligan took over from Mia Farrow who dropped out after becoming entangled in an unsavoury and emotionally draining child custody suit against her former partner, Woody Allen.

By early 1994, with *Wolf* yet to be seen, Pfeiffer was looking ahead for career moves and roles she might play. She was in the happy position of having most people in Hollywood in at least tacit agreement with Jonathan Demme's evaluation: 'As far as I'm concerned, the sky's the limit in what Michelle's capable of doing. It's hard for me to imagine anyone who, on a level of quality, would have the edge on her.'

The sky might be the limit but Pfeiffer's 'dark side' causes her to occasionally undermine such evaluations even if, at times, the impression is that she doesn't mean her words to be taken too literally: 'I've always wanted to play a realistic, no make-up, bag-lady. I've always been fascinated by bag-ladies who choose to live on the street. I've come to the point in my life where I can understand what makes them drop out. I've always been a worker, yet there is a part of me that feels I could end up like that too.'

While this might be the kind of feeling that overtakes many people, whether unsuccessful or highly successful, during moments when their darker side surfaces, in Pfeiffer's case, as with most people so struck by doubts and uncertainties, her commitment to her work keeps her from the reality of that desire for a different way of life. The depth of that commitment may be discerned from her heartfelt statement that 'there is nothing more exciting to me than getting the first draft of a script.'

And, as 1994 began, there was certainly no shortage of scripts, treatments, synopses, ideas, offers. Not that she would be rushed into incautious projects. Ed Limato, of International Creative Management, who had become her agent (he had first met Pfeiffer when he was with William Morris and had recommended her for *Scarface*) says of her that she is 'extremely bright. She's very quiet, she doesn't show it: but she's no fool.'

Aware of the financial possibilities arising from a reprise of her role as Catwoman, Pfeiffer said that she and Tim Burton, who had directed her in *Batman Returns*, 'would very much like to do a Catwoman movie and it all depends on whether we can get a script that we're happy with.'

In striking contrast to another whip-and-catsuit role, several current Pfeiffer-Guinzburg projects reveal a strong reflection of the current Hollywood love affair with classic American literature and the nation's cultural and historical heritage. The company has signed a development deal with Columbia to adapt Jane Smiley's Pulitzer Prize-winning novel, *A Thousand Acres*. A story about a farmer in the midwest and his three daughters, echoing the tragedy of King

Lear, the project was co-optioned with Jessica Lange's production company. In the trend, Lange starred in the 1992 film version of another American literary classic, Willa Cather's *O Pioneers!*

Then there is a contemporary staged version of Henry James's essay on the supernatural, *The Turn of the Screw* and two original screenplays; one is based upon the relationship between the artist Georgia O'Keefe and photographer Alfred Stieglitz, the other, which Kate Guinzburg states is 'a story about what happened to women when they got too much power,' is set during the Puritan witchcraft trials.

Another classic, but in a more popular sense, is yet another film stemming from a Cornell Woolrich novel. Unusually for this author, whose work is most often located in the times in which he wrote, *Waltz Into Darkness* is set in turn-of-the-century New Orleans and concerns the activities of a conwoman who poses as a mail-order bride. *Dear Digby* is the story of a letters editor on a feminist magazine, while another fourth-estate story is *Tabloid* which Pfeiffer has evolved with her close friend Cher. This deals with concerns about which both women have strong feelings; the erosion of privacy. The story concentrates upon a damaging conflict between an actress, a ruthless tabloid editor, and a young and still idealistic journalist whose beliefs run counter to the aims of the newspaper especially when it comes to invading the private life of a public figure.

Loss of privacy has become an unavoidable concomitant of fame in many fields, especially the motion-picture industry. Already it has driven Pfeiffer to live in a secluded and secure home. Kate Guinzburg says of her partner's attitude in business, 'I think Michelle sees good things in the world, but she expects the worst.' Perhaps the same might be said of her view of the world outside her carefully constructed hedge of privacy.

Long term, Pfeiffer has begun to wonder if the price to pay for privacy – something she clearly desires in her off-screen life and for her family – is to give up acting. Signs are there that this is much more than a casual notion born out of exasperation with the effect that fame has had upon her private life. Although she had been making, on average, two-and-a-half films a year, now she stated that she was 'aiming to do just one picture a year for a while'.

This could be a high price to pay (especially in monetary terms when she is presently estimated to earn $5.5 million per film), but for an intensely private person it might prove to be the only realistic solution. As Cher told *Rolling Stone*'s Gerri Hirshey, 'I have to shred my garbage now. Michelle is just starting to feel what its like to lose [her privacy]. I was famous when I was eighteen, so I knew it was part of my job description. Michelle is an *actress*. And she really doesn't want to give up that other part.'

Amongst other Pfeiffer-Guinzburg projects, and potentially one the most interesting, is a development of another Edith Wharton novel, *The Custom of the Country*, which was published in 1913. Adapted by Christopher Hampton, who wrote *Dangerous Liaisons*, this is the story of Undine Spragg, a ruthless social climber who sets out to use her physical beauty and sharp wits to exploit and plunder the society in which she lives. Without any emotional uncertainty, she marries calculatedly and then unceremoniously divorces in her pursuit of wealth and status only to be gradually overtaken by remorse.

In April 1994, while filming *My Posse Don't Do Homework* in California, she was offered the lead in a planned film version of *Evita*, the Andrew Lloyd Webber–Tim Rice musical. Despite the fact that the part had been rejected by Meryl Streep and Madonna, Pfeiffer was reportedly 'thrilled' at the prospect. Much less thrilled at the musical's depiction of Eva Peron were the people of Argentina. Early in June President Menem – leader of the ruling Peronista party – had to hastily withdraw his offer to director Oliver Stone of co-operation and support, to say nothing of the use of the Argentinian army as extras.

For all these many projects, however, there has been a slow

but certain emergence of elements of doubt about the future for Pfeiffer which are, perhaps, more noticeably realistic than her comments about the possibility of descent into the nether world of bag-ladies. Obviously, these centre upon her concern for privacy but also heavily feature her adoption of Claudia Rose which clearly affected her approach to life and her thinking about the future. To Leslie Bennetts, she said, 'By the time Claudia is school-age, I'll be very near forty, and they won't be hiring me much any more. Let's be realistic, things will have slowed down. I mean, look around. Our whole society is so geared toward youth . . . I have to think about my future, about retirement, about putting my child through school – and if I think my career is always going to be at this pinnacle, I'm crazy. I am very lucky to have had the wide range of opportunity I have in regard to the roles I play. At what point that starts to peter out, I don't know.' All this was said without any hint of frustration or resentment. Indeed, she added, 'I don't have anything to complain about, given the state of my career right now. I feel very fortunate.'

As for her private life, clearly this, too, was an area where she had nothing to complain about. And things were getting better. Unwittingly prophetic was a comment she made in her *Vanity Fair* interview when talking about her adoption of Claudia Rose. 'I want to have my own children too; I want to do both.'

Late in 1993, she was widely reported to have married David Kelley. Then, in January 1994, shortly after she pulled out of a film with Richard Gere, came an announcement of an event which statistically happens rather often to women after they have adopted a child. She was pregnant, something which took by surprise even those with ears closest to Hollywood's gossip ground.

In the circumstances, when the Oscar nominations came in mid-February, Michelle Pfeiffer probably thought, with good reason, that they were really rather unimportant.

However unimportant they might have been to Pfeiffer,

they must also have been very disappointing to many of the people with whom she had worked on *The Age of Innocence*.

For all the hype and insider gossip, and despite the film's undoubted excellence in so many aspects of its making, *The Age of Innocence* was not amongst the nominations for Best Picture. What was more, and perhaps even more surprising, Martin Scorcese was not a nominee as Best Director. Daniel Day-Lewis *was* nominated as Best Actor, but for *In the Name of the Father*, not for *The Age of Innocence*. And Michelle Pfeiffer was not nominated as Best Actress. The film picked up only four nominations, Winona Ryder as Best Supporting Actress, Art Direction, Screenplay Adaptation, and, the solitary success, Gabriella Pescucci for Costume Design.

Steven Spielberg, so often overlooked in the past, was not only nominated as Best Director for *Schindler's List* but also saw the film pick up a further eleven nominations, including Best Picture. It turned out to be Spielberg's year. *Schindler's List* collected seven Academy Awards including Best Director and Best Picture. To ice the cake brightly, Spielberg also saw his *Jurassic Park* win three Oscars.

However disappointed all those connected with *The Age of Innocence* must have been, for Michelle Pfeiffer the future was looking bright. Her private life had so far brought her all that she could have wished for, and if her career should stop here then it would still be a fairy-tale ending, the kind a Hollywood screenwriter of bygone days would have happily committed to paper. But these are different times and Pfeiffer is a different kind of woman to those portrayed in the women's pictures of the 1930s and '40s.

With the spirit of such past giants as Bette Davis and Katharine Hepburn to inspire her she can, if she chooses, continue with her acting career. Age will almost certainly not wither her. She has stated on several occasions that face-lifts and other standard ploys to fend off natural ageing processes are not for her. Anyway, they are unlikely to prove necessary – her bone structure will surely see to that. In any event, as she has conclusively proved in film after film, fundamentally she has always been a *character* actress, even when she has played the leading role, and there will never be any shortage of work for a character player of her quality.

But acting is not the only possible way ahead. If the demands of her new family and her concern over her privacy prove to be overwhelming, there are many other areas of the film-making process for her to explore.

Already, her power and the strength of the Pfeiffer Guinzburg portfolio of projects – allied to the hard core of realism that underpins her attitude towards her career and her life – means that her professional future can be anything she chooses it to be. She has already acted and produced; what next? Writing? Directing? It is hard to believe that she will settle for domesticity, however attractive that prospect might appear right now.

Of all activities in an uncertain world, making films must surely be one of the most fraught with hazards – from potholes to minefields. But if anything amidst such uncertainties can be thought of as a sure thing, it is that the world of motion pictures will see and hear a great deal more from the California check-out girl who made the magical journey to Hollywood and not only lived to tell the tale but also achieved phenomenal success.

The Michelle Pfeiffer story isn't finished yet.

Filmography

FANTASY ISLAND (1977-82) (Television)
ABC/Spelling-Goldberg: 2 x 95 mins + 120 x 50 mins in
colour. *Leading Players:* Ricardo Montalban, Herve Vil-
lachaize. Michelle Pfeiffer appeared in one episode in 1979.

DELTA HOUSE (1979) (Television)
Universal Television: 30-min. episodes, in colour. *Director:*
Alan Myerson. *Leading Players:* Peter Fox, Stephen Furst,
Bruce McGill, Lee Wilkof, Michelle Pfeiffer.

THE SOLITARY MAN (1979) (Television)
CBS Television: 120 mins. *Producer:* John Conboy. *Director:*
John Llewellyn Moxey. *Screenwriter:* James Byrnes. *Photogra-
pher:* Robert L. Morrison in colour. *Music:* Jack Elliott. *Leading
Players:* Earl Holliman, Carrie Snodgrass, Nicholas Coster,
Lara Parker, Dorrie Kavanaugh, Michelle Pfeiffer.

FALLING IN LOVE AGAIN (video title: **IN LOVE**) (1980)
A Paul Production: 95 mins in Metrocolor. *Producers:* Steven
Paul, Patrick Wright. *Director:* Steven Paul. *Screenwriters:*
Steven Paul, Ted Allen, Susannah York. *Photographers:* Mi-
chael John Mileham, Dick Bush, Wolf Suschitzky. *Editors:*
Bud Smith, Douglas Jackson, Jackelin Cambas. *Music:* Michel
Legrand. *Leading Players:* Elliott Gould, Susannah York, Stu-
art Paul, Michelle Pfeiffer, Kay Ballard, Robert Hackman,
Tony O'Dell, Steven Paul, Todd Hepler, Herbert Rudley,
Marion McCargo.

THE HOLLYWOOD KNIGHTS (1980)
Polygram: 91 mins in Metrocolor. *Producer:* Richard Lederer.
Director: Floyd Mutrux. *Screenwriter:* Floyd Mutrux. *Photog-*

rapher: William A. Fraker. *Leading Players:* Fran Drescher, Leigh French, Randy Gormel, Sandy Helberg, Gary Graham, Michelle Pfeiffer, Tony Danza.

CHARLIE CHAN AND THE CURSE OF THE DRAGON QUEEN (1980)

ACP/JSP: 95 mins in Technicolor. *Producer:* Jerry Sherlock. *Director:* Clive Donner. *Screenwriters:* Stan Burns, David Axelrod. *Photographer:* Paul Lohmann . *Editors:* Walt Hannemann, Phil Tucker. *Music:* Patrick Williams. *Leading Players:* Peter Ustinov, Lee Grant, Angie Dickinson, Richard Hatch, Brian Keith, Roddy McDowall, Rachel Roberts, Michelle Pfeiffer.

B.A.D. CATS (1980)

ABC Television/Spelling-Cramer: 6 x 60 mins in colour. *Producer:* Everett Chambers. *Music:* Barry De Vorzon, Mundell Lowe, Andrew Kulberg. *Leading Players:* Steven Hanks, Asher Brauner, Michelle Pfeiffer, Vic Morrow, Jimmie Walker.

SPLENDOR IN THE GRASS (1981)

NBC/Warners: 96 mins in colour. *Producer:* Arthur Lewis. *Director:* Richard C. Sarafian. *Leading Players:* Melissa Gilbert, Cyril O'Reilly, Ned Beatty, Eva Marie Saint, Michelle Pfeiffer, Jim Young, Nicholas Pryor.

CALLIE AND SON (1981)

CBS/Hemdale/Heller/City Films/Motown Pictures: 135 mins in colour. *Producer:* Rosilyn Heller. *Director:* Waris Hussein. *Screenwriter:* Thomas Thompson. *Photographer:* Dennis A. Dalzell. *Music:* Billy Goldenberg. *Leading Players:* Lindsay Wagner, Jameson Parker, Dabney Coleman, Jay Garrett, Michelle Pfeiffer, John Harkins, James Sloyan, Andrew Prine.

THE CHILDREN NOBODY WANTED (1981)

CBS/Warners/Blatt-Singer: 120 mins in colour. *Director:* Richard Michaels. *Screenwriter:* Lee Watson. *Photographer:*

Reynaldo Villalobos. *Music:* Barry De Vorzon. *Leading Players:* Frederic Lehne, Michelle Pfeiffer, Barbara Barrie, Joe Turly, Noble Winningham, Matt Clark.

GREASE 2 (1982)
Paramount: 114 mins in Panavision and Metrocolor. *Producers:* Robert Stigwood, Allan Carr. *Director:* Patricia Birch. *Screenwriter:* Ken Finkleman. *Photographer:* Frank Stanley. *Editor:* John F. Burnett. *Music:* Louis St Louis. *Leading Players:* Maxwell Caulfield, Michelle Pfeiffer, Adrian Zmed, Christopher McDonald, Lorna Luft, Maureen Teefy.

SCARFACE (1983)
Universal: 169 mins in Panavision and Technicolor. *Producer:* Martin Bregman. *Director:* Brian De Palma. *Screenwriter:* Oliver Stone. *Photographer:* John A. Alonzo. *Editor:* Jerry Greenberg, David Ray. *Music:* Giorgio Moroder. *Leading Players:* Al Pacino, Steven Bauer, Michelle Pfeiffer, Mary Elizabeth Mastrantonio, Robert Loggia, Miriam Colon, F. Murray Abraham, Paul Shenar, Harris Yulin.

LADYHAWKE (1985)
Warner Brothers/20th Century-Fox: 121 mins in Technicolor. *Producers:* Richard Donner, Lauren Schuler. *Director:* Richard Donner. *Screenwriters:* Edward Khmara, Michael Thomas, Tom Mankiewicz. *Photographer:* Vittorio Storaro. *Editor:* Stuart Baird. *Music:* Andrew Powell. *Leading Players:* Matthew Broderick, Rutger Hauer, Michelle Pfeiffer, Leo McKern, John Wood, Ken Hutchison, Alfred Molina.

INTO THE NIGHT (1985)
Universal: 115 mins in Technicolor. *Producers:* George Folsey Jnr, Ron Koslow. *Director:* John Landis. *Screenwriter:* Ron Koslow. *Photographer:* Robert Paynter. *Editor:* Malcolm Campbell. *Music:* Ira Newborn. *Leading Players:* Jeff Goldblum, Michelle Pfeiffer, Richard Farnsworth, Irene Papas, Bruce McGill, Kathryn Harrold.

ONE TOO MANY (1985)
Highgate for ABC in colour: 20 mins. *Director:* Peter Horton.
Leading Players: Michelle Pfeiffer, Val Kilmer, Mare Winning-
ham, Lance Guest.

SWEET LIBERTY (1985)
Universal: 107 mins in colour. *Producer:* Martin Bregman.
Director: Alan Alda. *Screenwriter:* Alan Alda. *Photographer:*
Frank Tidy. *Editor:* Michael Economou. *Music:* Bruce
Broughton. *Leading Players:* Alan Alda, Michael Caine,
Michelle Pfeiffer, Bob Hoskins, Lise Hilboldt, Lillian Gish,
Saul Rubinek, Lois Chiles.

AMAZON WOMEN ON THE MOON (1986)
Universal: 85 mins in Technicolor. *Producer:* Robert K. Weiss.
Directors: John Landis, Joe Dante, Robert K. Weiss, Carl Got-
tlieb, Peter Horton. *Screenwriters:* Jim Mulholland, Michael
Barrie. *Photographer:* Daniel Pearl. *Leading Players* (Hospital
Sketch): Griffin Dunne, Michelle Pfeiffer, Peter Horton. Brian
Ann Zoccola.

TALES FROM THE HOLLYWOOD HILLS:
NATICA JACKSON (1987)
Zenith/KCET in colour: 55 mins. *Producers:* Kimberley My-
ers, David Loxton. *Director:* Paul Bogart. *Screenwriter:* Andy
Wolk. *Leading Players:* Michelle Pfeiffer, Brian Kerwin, Hec-
tor Elizondo, George Murdock, Holland Taylor, Gail
Youngs.

THE WITCHES OF EASTWICK (1987)
Warner Brothers/Guber-Peters: 118 mins in Panavision and
Technicolor. *Producers:* Neil Canton, Peter Guber, Jon Peters.
Director: George Miller. *Screenwriter:* Michael Cristofer from
the novel by John Updike. *Photographer:* Vilmos Zsigmond.
Editor: Richard Francis-Bruce. *Music:* John Williams. *Leading
Players:* Jack Nicholson, Cher, Susan Sarandon, Michelle
Pfeiffer, Veronica Cartwright, Richard Jenkins, Carel Struy-
cken.

MARRIED TO THE MOB (1988)
Orion/Mysterious Arts/Demme: 104 mins in DuArt colour. *Producers:* Kenneth Utt, Edward Saxon. *Director:* Jonathan Demme. *Screenwriters:* Barry Strugatz, Mark R. Burns. *Photographer:* Tak Fujimoto. *Editor:* Craig McKay. *Music:* David Byrne. *Leading Players:* Michelle Pfeiffer, Matthew Modine, Dean Stockwell, Mercedes Ruehl, Alec Baldwin, Trey Wilson.

TEQUILA SUNRISE (1988)
Warner Brothers/Mount: 115 mins in DeLuxe colour. *Producer:* Thom Mount. *Director:* Robert Towne. *Screenwriter:* Robert Towne. *Photographer:* Conrad L. Hall. *Editor:* Claire Simpson. *Music:* Dave Grusin. *Leading Players:* Mel Gibson, Michelle Pfeiffer, Kurt Russell, Raul Julia, J.T. Walsh.

DANGEROUS LIAISONS (1988)
Warner Brothers: 120 mins in Eastman color. *Producers:* Norma Heyman, Hank Moonjean. *Director:* Stephen Frears. *Screenwriter:* Christopher Hampton from his play, *Les Liaisons Dangereuses. Photographer:* Phillipe Rousselot. *Editor:* Mick Audsley. *Music:* George Fenton. *Leading Players:* Glenn Close, John Malkovich, Michelle Pfeiffer, Swoosie Kurtz, Keanu Reeves, Mildred Natwick, Uma Thurman.

THE FABULOUS BAKER BOYS (1989)
Gladden Entertainment: 113 mins in DeLuxe colour. *Producers:* Paula Weinstein, Mark Rosenberg, Sydney Pollack. *Director:* Steve Kloves. *Screenwriter:* Steve Kloves. *Photographer:* Michael Ballhaus. *Editor:* Bill Steinkamp. *Music:* Dave Grusin. *Leading players:* Jeff Bridges, Michelle Pfeiffer, Beau Bridges.

THE RUSSIA HOUSE (1990)
Pathé: 123 mins in Technicolor. *Producers:* Paul Maslansky, Fred Schepisi. *Director:* Fred Schepisi. *Screenwriter:* Tom Stoppard from the novel by John Le Carré. *Photographer:* Ian Baker. *Editor:* Peter Honess. *Music:* Jerry Goldsmith. *Leading Players:* Sean Connery, Michelle Pfeiffer, Roy Scheider, James

Fox, John Mahoney, Michael Kitchen, J.T. Walsh, Klaus Maria Brandauer.

FRANKIE AND JOHNNY (1991)
Paramount: 113 mins in Technicolor. *Producer:* Garry Marshall. *Director:* Garry Marshall. *Screenwriter:* Terrence McNally from his own stage play. *Photographer:* Dante Spinotti. *Editors:* Battie Davis, Jackelin Cambas. *Music:* Marvin Hamlisch. *Leading Players:* Al Pacino, Michelle Pfeiffer, Hector Elizondo, Nathan Lane, Kate Nelligan, Jane Morris.

BATMAN RETURNS (1992)
Warner Brothers: 126 mins in Technicolor. *Producers:* Denise Di Novi, Tim Burton. *Director:* Tim Burton. *Screenwriter:* Daniel Waters. *Photographer:* Stefan Czapsky. *Editors:* Chris Lebenzon, Bob Badami. *Music:* Danny Elfman. *Leading Players:* Michael Keaton, Danny De Vito, Michelle Pfeiffer, Christopher Walken, Michael Gough, Michael Murphy, Cristi Conaway, Pat Hingle.

LOVE FIELD (1992)
Orion/Pfeiffer-Guinzburg: 138 mins in DeLuxe color. *Producers:* Sarah Pillsbury, Midge Sanford. *Director:* Jonathan Kaplan. *Screenwriter:* Dan Roos. *Photographer:* Ralf Bode. *Editor:* Jane Kurson. *Music:* Jerry Goldsmith. *Leading Players:* Michelle Pfeiffer, Dennis Haysbert, Brian Kerwin, Louise Latham, Stephanie McFadden, Peggy Rea, Beth Grant.

THE AGE OF INNOCENCE (1993)
Columbia: 138 mins in Technicolor. *Producer:* Barbara De Fina. *Director:* Martin Scorcese. *Screenwriters:* Jay Cocks, Martin Scorcese, from the novel by Edith Wharton. *Photographer:* Michael Ballhaus. *Editor:* Thelma Schoonmaker. *Music:* Elmer Bernstein. *Leading Players:* Daniel Day-Lewis, Michelle Pfeiffer, Winona Ryder, Miriam Margolyes, Richard E. Grant, Stuart Wilson, Geraldine Chaplin, Michael Gough, Alexis Smith, Jonathan Pryce, Sîan Phillips, Mary Beth Hurt.

WOLF (1994)
Columbia. In colour. *Producer:* Douglas Wick. *Director:* Mike Nichols. *Screenwriters:* Jim Harrison, Wesley Strick. *Photographer:* Giuseppe Rotunno. *Editor:* Sam O'Steene. *Music:* Ennio Morricone. *Leading Players:* Jack Nicholson, Michelle Pfeiffer, Kate Nelligan, James Spader, Christopher Plummer, Eileen Atkins, Richard Jenkins.

Bibliography

Magazine articles consulted are referred to in the text. Useful reference books were:

Halliwell, Leslie, *Film Guide* (Paladin, various editions)

Katz, Ephraim, *The International Film Encyclopedia* (Macmillan, 1982)

Shipman, David, *The Great Movie Stars: the Independent Years* (Macdonald, 1991)

Monthly Film Bulletin

Other books consulted and recommended as interesting further reading are:

Rosen, Marjorie, *Popcorn Venus* (Peter Owen, 1975)

Tims, Hilton, *Emotion Pictures: the 'Women's Picture', 1930-55* (Columbus, 1987)

Wharton, Edith, *The Age of Innocence* (Virago, 1988)

Index